This book was donated to us.
Please treat it as the gift it is.

"There is more treasure in books than in all the
pirate's loot on Treasure Island." ~ Walt Disney

ALSO BY AMY WILENSKY

Passing for Normal

the weight of it

the weight of it

a story of two sisters

AMY WILENSKY

HENRY HOLT AND COMPANY
NEW YORK

Henry Holt and Company, LLC
Publishers since 1866
115 West 18th Street
New York, New York 10011

Henry Holt® is a registered trademark of
Henry Holt and Company, LLC.

Library of Congress Cataloging-in-Publication Data
Wilensky, Amy S., date.
    The weight of it : a story of two sisters / Amy Wilensky.—1st ed.
    p. cm.
    ISBN 0-8050-7312-4
    1. Obesity—Psychological aspects. 2. Sisters—Family relationships.
I. Title.
RC552.O25W54 2004   2003056656
616.3'98—dc22

Henry Holt books are available for special promotions and
premiums. For details contact: Director, Special Markets.

First Edition 2004

Designed by Kelly S. Too

Printed in the United States of America

1   3   5   7   9   10   8   6   4   2

For Mormor, who taught us to make things ourselves, and that it mattered to do so; and for Johnson, my loyal, faithful friend

"Who are *you*?" said the Caterpillar.

This was not an encouraging opening for a conversation. Alice replied, rather shyly, "I—I hardly know, Sir, just at present—at least I know who I *was* when I got up this morning, but I think I must have been changed several times since then."

"What do you mean by that?" said the Caterpillar, sternly. "Explain yourself!"

"I can't explain *myself*, I'm afraid, Sir," said Alice, "because I'm not myself, you see."

"I don't see," said the Caterpillar.

"I'm afraid I can't put it more clearly," Alice replied, very politely, "for I can't understand it myself, to begin with; and being so many different sizes in a day is very confusing."

"It isn't," said the Caterpillar.

"Well, perhaps you haven't found it so yet," said Alice; "but when you have to turn into a chrysalis—you will some day, you know—and then after that into a butterfly, I should think you'll find it a little queer, won't you?"

"Not a bit," said the Caterpillar.

"Well, perhaps *your* feelings may be different," said Alice: "all I know is, it would feel very queer to *me*."

—LEWIS CARROLL

contents

the weight of it

prologue

"Whatever happens, don't let me eat any octopus," Alison announces, placing a small rectangular picnic basket on her tray table. A nervous flier, I have opted for the aisle seat in this row of three. Our cousin Jacy has requested, and been granted, the window, placing a chatty, highly caffeinated Alison smack dab in the middle. Although projected at a mere two hours and forty minutes, it is going to be a very long flight.

"Sure," says Jacy, after a moment's pause. "No problem on the octopus." Years of experience have taught us not to delve deeper. And in this case, it certainly isn't hard to agree. There is about as much chance of any of us encountering octopus during the upcoming week as there is of my catching some sleep on that plane. We are on a

7:00 a.m. flight, the first leg of our annual family vacation to North Captiva, a sparsely populated island off the gulf coast of Florida. There is only one restaurant on North Captiva, which we eat at for only one meal, and the menu item most closely approximating octopus is a grilled grouper sandwich, which in previous years Alison has eschewed, deeming lowly grouper not up to her culinary standards. The rest of our food we will buy at the Winn Dixie on the way to the boat taxi. If you have ever set foot in a Winn Dixie, and maybe even if you haven't, you can be quite sure it doesn't carry cephalopods.

As Alison pats the top of her basket with evident satisfaction, I close my eyes, gripping my book tightly. I hear her unlatch the clasp, poke around inside. Finally glancing over in spite of myself, I notice a small, sharp, delicate knife, which appears to be made of sterling silver. My father was forced to surrender his tiny Swiss army knife key chain before boarding, and a stern security guard had asked me to turn over my belt.

"How'd you get that on the plane?" I can't help asking, while checking to make sure no one around us has noticed.

"Oh, I have my ways," she smiles, holding the knife up so it glints under her overhead light. "I got other stuff through, too." I look over at Jacy, to determine if this, perhaps, is worth a little delving. A small shake of the head signals no, and we both turn our full attention, as usual, to Alison and—in this case—her picnic basket. She begins the unpacking. First, a cloth napkin. Next, homemade chocolate chip cookies wrapped individually in plastic wrap; a neat little container packed with port wine cheese; flatbreads in unusual shapes; colored goldfish crackers in a sealed pouch; Pellegrino for one; and that perfect little knife, which would not have been out of place on the side of a bone china plate at a formal afternoon tea. In fact, the whole spread seems vaguely British, wildly out of place in these surroundings, and so quintessentially Alison in so many ways that I feel, somehow, slightly peeved.

"They give you food on the plane, you know," I say, although a sufficient amount of time has passed that I am no longer certain this is true. As if on cue, the flight attendant approaching with the drink cart hands me three of the smallest bags of pretzels I have ever seen. Alison takes hers delicately between thumb and forefinger, with an expression of vague distaste.

"I prefer to travel with my own refreshment," she says for the benefit of everyone in earshot, depositing her pretzels by her feet.

"I'm going to the bathroom," I announce, suddenly feeling claustrophobic. There is a line at the nearest one, though, and because I mostly want distance from Alison, I walk back to where my parents are instead, but they are both asleep, and I don't feel like leaning over two strangers to wake them, especially when I don't have anything to say. The magazine bin at the back of the plane has been picked to the bone; there is nothing to do but return to my seat and ride out the trapped sensation I inevitably experience on airplanes, while Alison ostentatiously nibbles her way through canapés and sips seltzer beside me.

I trudge back up the aisle, eyes on the seats to my left. I stop short when I realize I have reached the front of the plane, cannot walk any further forward. Our row is in the middle, by an emergency exit; have I walked right by my own empty seat, somehow bypassed my sister and her elaborate display? The plane is only half full, but still I thought I'd been looking pretty carefully. I turn around, confused, scan the passengers' heads and shoulders for Alison's platinum braids.

"Are you okay?" a flight attendant asks, with a look that suggests if so, I should return whence I have come. I nod, distracted, and head down the aisle again, counting the rows to myself as I walk. This time I look for the picnic basket and stop in the proper place, but not without realizing what I have just done—walked right by my own sister and failed to recognize her.

My oversight shouldn't surprise me as much as it does, I suppose. In the summer of 2000, Alison—at 5 feet, 2 inches—weighed 317 pounds. Sitting next to me on the plane in the spring of 2003, she weighs 128. In well under three years, my sister lost almost two hundred pounds.

HAVE YOU EVER BEEN CAUGHT OFF GUARD BY YOUR OWN reflection, noticed a person in a mirror or store window and for just an instant not known it was you? This happened

to me once when I was in eighth grade, and I've never forgotten it. I was wearing a new outfit, a matching khaki-
colored jacket and pants that looked almost like a suit
and certainly unlike anything else I owned at the age of
fourteen. I was riding up an escalator in a shopping mall,
and dropped the bag I was holding on the step behind
me. I crouched to retrieve it, and when I stood up again, I
spotted a woman beside me, a small figure with a long
neck, dark hair smoothed back into a low ponytail, a
slight frown, and big, vague eyes. For a fraction of a second I thought: Who is she? When I realized what had
happened, I was consumed for the rest of the day by
wondering if the stranger I had seen in the mirror bore
any resemblance to the girl I was. The experience
reminded me of the first time I'd heard my voice on a
tape recorder and replayed it over and over again, thinking: that's not what I sound like; that can't be me. Like
my image in the mirror, it just didn't match what was
happening in my head.

   Almost every time I see Alison these days, or even
speak to her on the phone, I am reminded of the feeble
chestnut: the more things change, the more they stay the
same. I believe this is never truer than in families; a few
times I have heard my eighty-seven-year-old grandmother say, "Sandra!" in an uncharacteristically sharp
voice when my mother has displeased her somehow, and
felt a ripple in the time-space continuum so extreme that
my mother appears to me for a flash as a ten-year-old I
have seen only in a single photograph. And it holds true

for Alison, who is still in so many ways the same person she was at six, at fourteen, at twenty-two.

Whenever I'm with Alison now, I try to see us as an outsider would, playing off each other the way siblings often do, in a duet so flawless and yet so tired it hums like elevator music or a noise filter. I see this: two women in their early thirties, whose close relationship is evident in their nearly identical noses and voices, bone structure, high foreheads, and something about the shape of the eyes. Even when we are seated, though, it is clear I am taller, and I think it is clear that I am older, too, just slightly. This interaction, these physical qualities have always been true, as far back as my memory will take me. We *are* the same; our duet performed these days as though by player piano.

Except. Except for the fact that an outside observer can't see a past in which nothing and everything has changed. An observer can't see experience, or history, only the way people look, and the way Alison looks now is definitely not the way she looked for most of her life. I have been present during a number of recent encounters with old friends and acquaintances whose jaws drop when she says her name. I have observed eyes widen, heads scratched, glasses removed, polished, and replaced. Perhaps more jarring to me, I have seen the immense satisfaction in Alison's eyes when she registers this shock.

How did this transformation come to pass? At the age of twenty-nine, my sister underwent a gastric bypass surgery. The factors that led her to take this step are familiar to two thirds of the people in this country: her weight was affecting her health, and all her attempts to alleviate the problem failed and then exacerbated it, in the vicious circle fat people come to know like their own reflections. Why was Alison so fat, and how did she get that way? This is a question thin people love to ask about fat people in general, with sympathy or pity tinged with disgust, but it is not a question that particularly interests me. Alison was fat for a hundred reasons, the same one-of-a-kind, never-to-be-re-created mix of biology, environment, personality, and experience that makes each of us who we are, for better and for worse.

When we reached preadolescence and Alison began her jagged climb to her maximum weight, I remained small. As Alison—not helped by her lack of a growth spurt—grew larger, nobody mentioned a physical resemblance between us anymore or commented on Alison's appearance at all. When Alison lost and gained, lost and gained, over the course of her late adolescence and twenties, she experienced the fickle praise and implicit criticism of those who noticed the changes. I reached my adult height and weight at sixteen, and the latter hasn't changed much in seventeen years.

To those who don't know Alison well, her weight loss has marked a complete transformation, the external informing the internal, a Cinderella story with a simple, happy, eradicating end. Even those who do know her well—who were in her orbit as she gained all that weight, lost much of it several times over, lived primarily as a fat person for fifteen years, and finally lost it for what I think is for good—talk about her in the language of "before" and "after," as if she had lived two lives: a fat life first, and now a second, much more enjoyable one, in the thin body we all assume makes everything okay. I find this alternately perplexing and infuriating. Alison's weight was and remains so far down on my list of how I would describe her that it would come after "master Othello player," "makes her own fruit-infused vodkas," and "has an uncanny ability to find a parking spot in any city in the country." Perhaps this is hard to believe, considering the enormous role Alison's weight has played in my life and in our relationship. But before she is fat or thin, she is my sister, and if she had no arms and legs or went crazy or tattooed her face like a Maori warrior, the fact of our kinship would still trump it all. That's the crux of it, actually, that word: *sister.* Alison is my flesh and blood, the person whose genes most closely resemble my own, my sister before everything else, even if that means I see her most clearly in relation to me.

When you say a word over and over again, you eventually reach the point when it loses all meaning. When it rains continuously for four days, you forget exactly how it feels to stand in the sun. And when you spend the first eighteen years of your life several feet away from somebody who shares your nose, your voice, your handwriting, your memories—who knows your made-up words and what you would order at a diner down to the extra cup of gravy for the well-done fries—what you see is not a shape at all; in fact, it isn't even corporeal.

For years I had watched people watch Alison, wary and suspicious. I had come to expect people to disparage her in some way, shoot her a dirty look, eye her with false pity or scorn. At some point over the past three years, I have stopped watching in this way, shrugged off the broiling mixture of protectiveness and anger, empathy and shame. Though Alison told me recently that she worries she will always feel as though the word *fat* is tattooed on her forehead, I am proof that she is wrong.

We wear our greatest scars on the inside, I think, all of us, and the scars themselves are as unique as our fingerprints, those intricate whorls we learn, early on, are signatures of a primal blueprint, a stamp that says: this is me and only me. If others can't see these scars, then we have a certain liberty to project anew, to tell only what we desire to share, to withhold what we need to protect. Before the scar, however, must come the wound. For Alison, obesity itself was an extended gash, shallow and painfully slow to close. It is a luxury for her to keep that word inside: *fat*— that word that once defined her to the outside world, that word that has become her scar. Like any scar, it cannot be erased, but it can fade and smooth out over time. Like any scar, it will always remind her—and me—of what happened before the healing.

A FEW YEARS AGO I WAS RUMMAGING AROUND IN MY parents' basement, a cavernous space packed floor to ceiling with ancient board games, unmatched suede boots from the 1970s, and life-size cardboard representations of Elvis, James Dean, and Marilyn Monroe. I was looking for something; I can't remember what. A book fell on my head, and I picked it up, wiping my dusty hands on my jeans. It was an unfamiliar cloth-bound journal, which seemed odd, for as far as I knew, I was the only member of my family who had even attempted to keep one. For a second I actually assumed it had to be mine, felt a pulse of anticipation at discovering a forgotten artifact from my childhood (generally the reason I rummage around in the basement at all).

When I let it fall open in the middle, however, I immediately recognized Alison's handwriting, so much like mine yet looser and loopier, as though I were writing overtired or in the semidark. Sometimes our writing is so similar that an outsider would not be able to tell whose is whose. I have always found this to be an odd genetic quirk: family resemblance not in what we say or write but in how we actually construct the words. Sometimes now I remind myself to watch Alison perform mundane tasks, such as scrape a bowl with a spatula or braid her hair without looking in a mirror, and trace the movement to find the inevitable shadow similarity.

I flipped through the journal, and my own name jumped out at me right away. Ethical dilemma: Should I read? I didn't mull over this question for long. Alison and Jacy, a month younger than Alison and her regular coconspirator throughout our childhood, had discovered all the hiding places I ever had for my own diaries, such as they were. Because I liked to write, I was often the recipient of those pastel-colored or floral-patterned versions with the effeminate miniature keys, and at first I would try to live up to the cheerful, girlish expectations of the giver and the diary itself. Although I'd never been truly comfortable writing down my private thoughts, Alison and Jacy, more so than the ill-suited format, were probably the leading factor in my eventual abandonment of the process altogether. Nosy and relentless is a deflating combination.

I sat down next to Elvis at one of my mother's colonial desks with the chair attached and started in. After a few minutes, my face grew hot. Apparently Alison had kept this journal during the trip we took to Sweden one summer with my mother and grandmother when Alison and I were in college. I wracked my brain, but I couldn't remember seeing her write in it, in spite of the fact that we shared a room for the duration of the trip and that she always fell asleep first. Very carefully I replaced the journal in its storage box, the box on its shelf beside a plastic container of seashells and a canvas bag out of which a few old dolls were listing, eyeless and half clothed. Uncharacteristically, I felt no desire to continue reading, although normally I would have, at the very least, skimmed the remaining pages for other sightings of my name. One of my parents' cats slithered around my ankle, glad for a companion in her preferred prowling spot, but I'd lost my taste for prowling and walked back up the stairs, remembering to turn off the lights behind me for a change.

Back home in New York, I found myself thinking about the journal entry as I followed my daily routine, especially as I got dressed in the mornings, even more so every time we spoke on the phone. But I didn't tell Alison what I had read. I didn't tell anyone, except one of my oldest friends, who knew us both, and who smiled a small smile and said only, in a way I found irritatingly loaded, "I didn't know Alison kept a journal."

The next time I was at my parents' house, I went back to the basement, ostensibly to find my missing tall black boots, which I suspected—based on previous comments indicating interest in them—were in Alison's closet in Boston. In truth, I hoped to stumble upon this journal again; it seemed important, somehow, to see the words in print, although I certainly hadn't forgotten them. I couldn't find it, though, so I have to reproduce her words as best I can. The italics—although perhaps this goes without saying—are mine.

She wrote, "Today we went to Dallarna, where they make the wooden horses, because Amy wanted to replace her clogs, the ones my mom bought her on her last trip here. My mom thought I would like some, too, and I did: I liked the red ones best, like Amy's, the ones she was replacing. When I was trying them on, though, Amy started telling me how much nicer the black ones were. She said she thought they were more 'me,' that they would go better with my clothes. She said that I would maybe not want to wear the red ones when we were home because they were so conspicuous. Finally, I was so sick of it I just agreed to get the black ones. I know exactly why Amy made me get the black ones. She wants to be the only one with the red ones because they're the coolest and because she'll get attention when she wears them, and it would take attention away from her if I had them, too. Whatever. I actually feel bad for her. Is there really anything sadder than thinking your whole *identity* is wrapped up in a pair of stupid *shoes?*"

When I look back on it now, I think that moment, in my parents' jam-packed basement with cobwebs in my hair and mouse droppings all over my socks, was the first time I saw Alison as wholly separate from myself. I certainly wouldn't say that, until that moment, I had viewed us as inextricably linked, or as two halves of a whole, or any of the things sisters tend to say about each other in television movies or on greeting cards. It's more as if I suddenly realized, after twenty-five years, that Alison had her own perspective on our shared experiences (and also that she had my number).

Identity has always been a particular obsession of mine: how we get it, what can shake it, why it matters, what it means. I have always believed mine to be inherently solid, in ways both good and bad, often feel so unshakably myself that I want to scream. Unlike many other people, those who have known Alison all her life and those who met her later on, at any stage, I have also considered Alison's pretty well set in stone. To me, the drastic shifting of her shape over the years, from very small to very large to very small again, has only revealed the immutability of its contents.

Emerson himself, the quintessential transcendentalist, wrote, "We live amid surfaces, and the true art of life is to skate well on them." Maybe we are what we see. Maybe we are who we see reflected in other people's eyes. One thing is for sure: when my sister lost almost two hundred pounds, the way she was seen by the rest of the world was what changed most of all. If there has been any change in Alison's essential self, I think it is best expressed when she meets a smiling face and has to question, on some level, just how she earned that smile. Most of us take common decency for granted, assume that a greeting earns you one back by virtue of your membership in what we call humanity. Most of us have no occasion to question every innocuous gesture or to appreciate the heartfelt ones that can seem hard to come by. But to be obese in our society at this point in history—regardless of the fact that you are in a growing majority—is to be so visible as to be invisible, to go unseen.

When I first read Alison's journal entry from that Sweden trip, years before she became the size I think she was meant to be, it struck me, too, how differently the two of us had formed our respective identities, how in so many ways we had been given no choice. I never would have imagined she could have summed me up so quickly and accurately, so dismissively, really, in such a damning handful of words. It was true, of course, every word. I had wanted desperately to be the only one with the showy red clogs, which had given me nicknames at school and smiles on the street, and I had been certain that Alison had been convinced, hook, line and sinker, by my crafty powers of persuasion. Instead, she had seen right through me (had she always?) and once again accepted her physical role offstage. I hadn't realized how much she didn't need to see her name at the top of the program to feel as if she had a part in the play. I had never acknowledged to myself how much I did.

More so than anyone else I know, Alison does not care what other people think about her. This is both a rare gift and a heavy burden, too, particularly to those around her, but there is no question in my mind that her attitude stems from the years she spent in a body that betrayed her, that did not feel like her own. If you have to surrender ego, it eventually creeps away on its own, to be replaced by something else less easy to define. Starting in adolescence, when appearance begins its trek toward omnipotence, Alison did not have the option to define herself by the way she looked, or rather she became defined entirely by her looks, depending on your point of view. When people looked at her at all—and most people look away when someone is obese, after first registering "fat" in their heads (and often on their faces)—they looked right through.

Alison knew, years before I ever stopped to think about it, that it didn't really matter what color shoes she wore—it wouldn't have the slightest effect on how she was perceived by other people. We may think we are the shoes on our feet, the shallow little quirks we hope will make us special, let us stand out from the crowd, but she knew, and knows now, in a different way from most of us, that to the world at large we *are* the faces and bodies we see reflected back at us in mirrors, store windows, and the eyes of the people we meet as we walk—blessedly light or unfairly weighted down—through every single day.

Privately, I have a theory, and I think that Alison has taught it to me. There's a lot of weight to the things we never say, and I wanted to say them, most of all for Alison herself. So this is it, the theory, and most days I think it's true: the less you think about how other people see you, the more clearly you come to see yourself. If you can do that—even touch the outer edge of it while standing on your toes—we think you can do anything at all.

O N E

two of us

We grew up in the suburbs, and our pediatrician's office was in Boston, a good half hour's drive from our house. Once a year my mother would take us in for our check-ups, an outing I regarded with equanimity, even looking forward to the likely, exhilarating spectacle of a temper tantrum thrown by a younger child in the packed waiting room, the lollipops presented at the end of the appointment, and a possible stop at Downtown Crossing or Fanueil Hall. I remember the ride in: the thrill of heading into the city, even for such a prosaic purpose; the serene little world the three of us made in my mother's small car, passing the looming Children's Hospital, where we knew dying children were sent; and the straight shot up the ancient elevator to a high floor where overburdened nurses and lousy *Highlights* magazines awaited.

At the doctor's office we had our eyes and ears checked, throats swabbed, knees knocked, temperatures taken, and measurements recorded on a piece of paper Dr. Hubbell kept on a clipboard, which also held similar pieces of paper from previous years. The appointments themselves blend together so seamlessly that I remember only one with any specificity; it was the year I was in fifth grade, and I must have been ten. I was forty-eight inches tall, and I weighed forty-eight pounds, a coincidence that struck me as meaningful, as though I was destined to have a lucky year, some uncanny good fortune. I was a child who appreciated—and found comfort in—symmetry and order. What it actually meant was that I was unusually small for my age, four feet tall and under fifty pounds. Dr. Hubbell showed me the height and weight chart as he explained this to my mother; then, a competitive kid, I was dismayed by how low my percentiles were, naively assuming they were like grades: higher was better. To myself, I pledged to grow, to do stretching exercises and eat more, the initial pleasure in my matching height and weight floating out the window grate and down to the grimy parking garage below. Then I noticed Alison's chart still out, as the doctor and my mother rambled on about strep throat season and ear infections. She had seen the doctor first that day. Her height percentile was down in my range, which made sense, as she was always about two inches shorter than I. Her weight was not. It was much

higher than mine, and I noticed this, not impressed or disparaging, but neutral, as I approached the doctor's office
itself, simply taking note. Alison wasn't fat, she wasn't
thin, she was just Alison. Back in the car, though, as we
sucked contemplatively on our lollipops, I decided not to
tell Alison about my matching forty-eights, but I wasn't
sure why.

MASKING TAPE DOWN THE MIDDLE OF THE CAR'S BACK
seat—does this mean anything to you? If you are an only
child, or one of twelve, probably not. I have a hunch,
however, that it could serve as a metaphor for the line
that divides the lives of siblings other than Alison and me.
I'm not certain we ever marked this essential separation
with actual tape, but it doesn't really matter. Throughout
our childhood—and way too far into adolescence—there
may as well have been a laser beam splitting the car, any
car, in half, a beam that—if so much as inadvertently
elbowed—would shock the body attached to the offend-
ing elbow right back into her designated corner. When I
think of how many hours and with what emotional fervor
I guarded my side—well, let's just say it's a good thing
there wasn't a third child around. And I don't even want
to get into the particulars of the system devised for those
exhilarating occasions when the front seat was free, but
I will make a shameful confession: on even-numbered
days, I still feel a faint but unmistakable thrill when I sink
down next to the driver.

When Alison was born, I was thirteen months old, but in that thirteen months I had managed to stake a firm claim to every square inch of my parents' attention, a claim I have never successfully relinquished. This seems to be universal among older children, who after the initial glory days forever attempt to reclaim their birth status in one way or another. It is no accident, in other words, that Cain, perhaps the world's most notorious oldest sibling, committed fratricide. When Alison was born, I took out my hostility, Cain-like, directly on the source of the shift and have been struggling with the impulse ever since.

Apparently when Alison was just a few months old, I was caught trying to turn her out of her cradle. A picture exists, in fact, of me standing over the cradle, angelic in short-lived curls and a long white nightgown, looking lovingly down on what the image suggests is my new baby sister. I can only imagine that this photograph was snapped under the watchful eye of one of my parents or grandparents, and that moments later, when this justifi-ably anxious adult turned to answer a telephone or open a window, I made my move—the first of many—to unseat the interloper I hadn't asked for and didn't want.

Of course I have no memory of Alison being born, no recollection of the thoughtful, sensible talks and books parents give first children to prepare them for the upheaval to come, although I'm sure I had both in spades. I do have a vague and fuzzy and probably false memory of being presented with the enormous stuffed dog my aunt bought me as compensation for the indignity my parents had brought home as blithely as one would a bag of groceries or a lamp. This giant dog now sits in a corner of my father's den and may serve him as a warm reminder of this period in his life when his family felt complete. When *I* look at it, I get a tiny shiver down my spine, as though sensing somehow that the heavy ceiling beams of this part of the house are about to loosen, fall squarely on my head.

Irish twins, I believe, is the politically incorrect term for children born as close together as we were. And in fact, for the first seven or eight years of our lives people usually thought we were twins, identical twins even, although I was always taller, and Alison didn't have freckles. Alison and I liked this extra attention and voluntarily dressed alike, chose matching ribbons for our braids, and cocked our heads to the right in the same stagy way in many of our holiday card pictures. In photographs from these years in which you cannot see our faces, the only way to tell us apart is the length of our hair, my braids or ponytails inching slightly further down my back than hers.

Sometimes I dream that we are seven and eight again in Alison's pink-carpeted closet, wrapped in our favorite cats-in-sneakers sleeping bags and eating penny candy while she indulges me by letting me read aloud to her from the *Five Little Peppers*, not in my schoolmarmy, show-off reading voice but in my real one, with variations for the characters: high-pitched and girlish for Phronsie, low and growly for the boys. Picture us in that closet: we are tiny, have straight bangs across our foreheads, round cheeks, identically formed hands and feet. Picture Alison falling asleep: first, head bobbing ever so slightly, then eyelids drooping, chin lowering to chest with every audible inhalation, until I flick her sharply on the crown of her head with my forefinger.

"I'm reading," I admonish, "stay awake," and she either nods, so drowsy she doesn't even know what I'm saying, or yells at me to get out of her room right that second and take my stupid sleeping bag with me.

Finally, picture me, woefully unappreciated, a classical Greek orator in my own mind, reading the *Five Little Peppers* alone under the covers with a flashlight in my own bedroom with its narrow, ordinary closet not big enough for a single sleeping bag, let alone two. I am sulking, wondering how I can get Alison to forgive me and let me come back—with the book—without surrendering my all-important pride. That's the problem with reading out loud: there's really no point if you don't have an audience, and Alison always was—still is—my best one.

IF I'M CERTAIN OF ANYTHING, IT IS THIS: YOUR SIBLINGS are the only other citizens from a country nobody else will ever visit. Adults like childhood generalized, expanded to a fuzzy, falsely unifying idea made up of equal parts nostalgia and multicolored crayons, but childhood itself is painfully, excruciatingly specific, and few other people can ever come close to understanding your own. Parents are ambassadors from another place entirely; they think they understand the language, the dress code, the culture, but they are always off beat and a few steps back, mocked by the natives whenever they walk out of the room. They hail from their own countries; if you watch them with their own siblings, this realization will make you feel strange and even a little afraid, as though you're walking near a minefield or have ventured into forbidden territory with no idea how to get back home. Occasionally a glimpse of your parents with their siblings will provide insight into your relationship with your own, an insight along these lines: oh my God, it never changes. She'll be like this when she's 110.

My own parents are both oldest children. They were determined to raise their two children fairly, like equals, and perhaps it is typical of oldest children to be wildly naive about fairness and equality. From the very beginning, for example, Alison refused to conform to my ideas of what a younger sister should be; more frustrating still, from the very beginning she refused to conform to any expectations at all. When Alison was a baby and then a toddler, in our first house, she had a tiny bedroom, consumed almost entirely by her crib, a room intended as a pantry or a walk-in closet. Whereas I had always been a stationary sleeper, Alison hated that crib and quickly learned to extricate herself from it, regardless of preventive measures taken after her initial escape. Among my earliest memories are snippets of conversation between my parents regarding Alison's ferocious pursuit of freedom and attendant lack of fear.

Unself-conscious from the start as well, Alison liked to sing to herself, songs of her own devising, during those moments when she wasn't engaged in fleeing her crib. I have a much clearer memory of her voice, faintly audible all the way to my bigger pink room at the other end of the house, as she serenaded her menagerie of stuffed animals with a particular favorite: "Froggies on the Lily Pad." Like many of her compositions, this one was composed solely of the title words belted out in an endless loop in her distinctive, tuneless, joyful style.

Partly because I was certain in my likes and dislikes, all of which had come first by definition, Alison became even more so in hers. And partly because I jumped all over her if I so much as suspected she was copying me, her tastes became more creative and daring than mine. Once when we were coloring together in the intricate design books my mother bought us (now, I suspect, because to finish a single page took hours of intense concentration), I finished a particularly elaborate design that had required the painstaking filling-in of hundreds of tiny triangles and diamonds with the finest-tipped markers we owned. I assessed my work and was proud; my color scheme featured shades of blue, from navy to a sky blue nearly white, and the results were perfect. I had not miscolored a single shape, and no color bled beyond the spidery lines of the pattern. Ready to receive my admiration due, I cleared my throat and looked over at Alison, turning my design to face her, so she could see—and feel jealous of—my speed and prowess, the utter superiority of my work. She didn't look up, though, and I noticed her tongue was slightly out, wedged in the corner of her mouth, which meant she was completely immersed. Occasionally I did this too, as she had pointed out when I teased her about it, but she did it all the time.

Involuntarily, I pulled my design back toward me, shielding it slightly with my arm. Alison was not coloring in the design the way you were supposed to. She was not filling in each tiny triangle or diamond with one color, and the ones around it with different colors, so that no two shapes of the same color would touch, which I had considered the primary goal of the process. Instead, she had found larger patterns in the small ones, had filled in whorls and stars in a rainbow of colors, lots of shapes together to create them, and had blacked out the little shapes remaining in between with an ordinary black marker, the kind my father brought home from his office for addressing mail. The effect was kaleidoscopic in a way the author of these design books had probably never dreamed a child would discover. It looked as though she'd strewn a handful of gemstones against a nighttime sky, and even her mistakes glinted appealingly against their blackest backdrop.

"What?" she said, finally feeling my eyes not on her work but on her small round face. The tongue retreated. "Oh, you're finished," she said, a little deflated, trying to get a look at my work. "I hope you didn't use up all the blues."

"You're doing it wrong," I said with all the flat affect I could muster, getting up from the table and taking my design with me, although at that moment I wanted nothing more than to scrunch it up and bury it in the trash.

It wasn't just art projects that Alison stamped with her personal touch; it was everything she owned. I'm not sure from whom she inherited her Mae West philosophy, as neither of my parents are prone to grand-scale accumulation, but Alison has always believed that "too much of a good thing is marvelous," or "mahhhvelous," as she herself would say. There was a period back when Robin Leach was still on television when she liked telling people— friends, family, total strangers at the grocery store—that she had "champagne tastes and caviar dreams," which always made me feel like hiding my head in my sweater, but other people seemed to think it was pretty funny coming from a kid in pigtails, and I couldn't deny that it was true. While I organized and reorganized my books by category and made sure my dolls' clothes were spick-and-span, Alison launched the first of her many collections: teddy bears. Lots of kids collect things, and I did, too, but I never encountered anyone else who collected on Alison's scale. Before we moved out of our first house, her bears and their differently specied relations were threatening to force her into the kitchen to sleep. Once she had her own larger room in our new house, the bears multiplied like rabbits, if you will, until there were so many bears, and so much bear-related paraphernalia, that they had to be played with in shifts, for Alison was not the sort of collector who was after sheer quantity—she actually wanted to play with the bears, and she had devotion enough for them all.

There was nothing Alison owned that could not be taken along wherever she went, which was more or less convenient and charming depending on the setting in question. Our Jewish father and Lutheran mother had decided to send us to a Unitarian Sunday school to learn about different religious traditions and to be exposed to a consistent and questioning spiritual influence, along with other children from open-minded families; fortunately the church we attended allowed not just children of mixed marriages but also giant bagfuls of their stuffed animals each week. When I think of Alison and me at church, I think of us under the enormous horse chestnut tree on the front lawn, a tree that has stood in Sudbury Center since before the United States was a country, surrounded by a dozen kids who wanted to see what Alison had in her bags.

What *did* Alison have in her bags? First, there were the bears, usually the extended family of small ones, the Steiff bears with the gold tags in their ears that stand about three inches high but have arms and legs with joints and are thus afforded a certain dignity other miniature animals are not. Alison's bears were always nicely turned out for excursions, in sweaters my grandmother had knit them or clothes Alison had sewn herself, never as carefully as the outfits I made for my dolls and stuffed animals but always in more fashionable, daring styles. After the bears came the art supplies: colored pencils in a case shaped like a giant pencil itself, with a cap you turned to make the appropriate color fall out; Magic Markers in sets of a hundred, which I organized from lightest to darkest but Alison used so frequently she couldn't be bothered; and notebooks of all shapes and sizes, which could be used for starting a club at a moment's notice or for taking notes on an impromptu spy mission, of which I was often the unwitting subject.

It wasn't just to church that Alison carried her supplies; it was everywhere—to family dinners, to school each morning, and even for a short ride in the car up the street. (I'm not sure if this was a security measure or a practical one, but it has continued to this day. Last year Alison took the bus from Boston to visit me in New York for two days and brought along not just four substantial pieces of luggage but also beef tenderloin for twelve, a quart of blood orange concentrate, two dozen tart shells, and her own squeeze bottles "for plating," because, as she explained, "I knew you wouldn't have the right kind." I didn't tell her I wasn't certain what "plating" meant.) My mother used to drive us to elementary school in her beloved MG convertible, and a couple of teachers and administrators would often emerge from the front offices to watch us pile out of the car—the spectacle would not have been half so exciting if in addition to the two of us, our cellos, and our schoolbags, Alison had not unloaded—at least on occasion—her bear house, electronic Simon game, sticker albums, and a couple of dress-up outfits in a red metal doll trunk.

ALTHOUGH ALISON REFUSED TO CONFORM TO MY expectations—openly adoring and worshipful like Beth to my role model Jo in *Little Women* was the sort of thing I had in mind—she was still my little sister, and usually I could get her on board if she wasn't engaged with a friend or with Jacy. While I played with Jacy's brothers, Andy and Brandon—Whiffle ball, fort building, or club launching—Alison and Jacy immersed themselves in more traditional (for girls anyway) imaginative play. If the game was House, then Andy and I would join in, seduced by the opportunity to enact the roles of parents. I would also agree to be the teacher in a game of School if Andy and Brandon weren't around, although Alison and Jacy usually saw through this offer pretty quickly and declined before I could bring out my handcrafted, extra-challenging workbooks; I relished correcting my students' errors with a new red pen. Their favorite game, after Orphans, was Sisters—although I didn't know about this one until we were nearly adults. Sisters was played when I was not around and clearly tapped into some well of need in both Alison and Jacy, sandwiched as she was between two boys. This I understood. Alison, however, had a sister—me.

It was also clear that I didn't conform to Alison's idea of the perfect older sister—who in children's literature is usually smug, superior, and condescending, albeit protective.

Still, when Alison and I were alone, we occasionally far surpassed the sum of both our parts. Much as our parents, who are extremely different from each other, have rounded out each other's hollows and edges, Alison's resourcefulness, generous nature, and refusal to get mired down in the details tempered my perfectionism, anxious nature, and tendency to spread myself so thin I became transparent, leaving patchy stamp collections, unfinished poetry volumes, and half-made quilts in my wake. On the flip side, my grand plans and ceaseless energy often prodded Alison to create when she might have observed or gone along for the ride; regardless, my drive to control and hers to please and impress began early, intensified in rivalry, and have, in some ways, become very useful to us both.

When I think back now, I am amazed by the scale on which we carried out some of our ideas. Many of our games encompassed little worlds, whose planning and maintaining played to both our strengths. Once, at the Concord toy shop, we saw a wooden educational toy that involved dropping a marble into a hole and watching as it launched a number of elaborate systems involving levers, the domino effect, magnets, and other elements of physics. When we got home, I announced to Alison that we would build a life-size version in our backyard. Probably Alison was the one who decided it would facilitate operations if we were to downsize the structure to doll size, but even so, the results involved the picnic table, both benches, the space trolley, a good fifty yards of rope, and enough baskets to fill a Mexican market stall. The project took us several weeks to complete, and I'm sure there were any number of occasions on which one of us was not speaking to the other over a design dispute. But when we put the first hapless doll in the launching basket and watched as our hard work set off the chain reaction we'd envisioned, our shared, silent satisfaction was worth every minute of effort, every time I'd had to bite my tongue and, I suspect, every time she'd had a piece of the works removed from her hands so it could be "fixed" by me.

One of our ventures proved to be financially reward-ing as well as morally instructive—for me anyway. The summer we were ten and eleven, at the height of the preppy clothing craze, we decided to make our own bar-rettes like the ones in stores, so we could have as many different kinds and colors as we wanted. My mother had turned our basement into a crafts room, and we had drawers and shelves full of art supplies, including dozens of types of ribbon, from satin to grosgrain. We started to experiment and soon had friends begging for the reject sets and asking if they could commission us to make pairs for a certain outfit, bat mitzvah, or upcoming dance.

After a few weeks we arrived at an unspoken agree-ment: Alison would make streamers, in which two colors of very thin satin ribbon were woven around the barrette itself and at which she was faster and neater than I was (although I would never have admitted this), and I would make a style my mother had designed, with three loops of wider ribbon in descending sizes, tiered and glued to sim-ulate a fancy bow. Competition and a shared obsessive tendency spurred us on to great heights of productivity, and soon we had so many barrettes that we could not give them away fast enough, in spite of the constant demands of our friends.

One day, soon after we'd arrived on Martha's Vineyard, where we spent each August, someone suggested that we could try to sell our barrettes to some of the boutiques in Edgartown and Vineyard Haven, that it might be a good way to learn about starting a business and keeping financial records, as well as earn some money of our own. We jumped on this idea, and with the help of our endlessly accommodating grandparents (I will never forget the sight of my self-contained grandfather carefully sorting precut ribbon into piles of pink and lavender), built up supplies of our respective products. With advice and input from our parents—my mother had suggested we make a display case to bring along, my father talked sales technique of the "you never get a second chance to make a first impression" variety—we were dropped off at the first store on our list while my father went to park the car. I don't actually remember our pitches, although I'm sure we were nervous and flustered, but I probably introduced us to the sales clerk and asked if we could talk to the owner; there were many times throughout our childhood that I took the role of leader because we both assumed I would, no matter how ill suited I was to the task at hand. What I do remember is the aftermath, the ride back to the house, our display cases on our laps, the heavy silence in the car.

Because the streamer barrettes were ubiquitous that summer, this particular boutique did not require any more stock at the time, the owner explained, treating us very professionally, as perhaps we had not anticipated. However, the bow variety, the style I was making from my mother's design, was not as common, and the owner would be interested in trying some of them. In the heat of the moment it was all I could do to make the arrangements, take down her order, and agree to her delivery date. As soon as we were out of the store, though—with tourists in pink sweaters and Bermuda shorts laughing and talking as they passed us on the sidewalk—I became painfully aware of Alison's hot disappointment and the anger that radiated from her small person. For a moment the surprised pleasure was knocked right out of me. It was not the first time one of us had "won" something the other did not, but in the past we had not usually been competing for just the same thing. Suddenly I found myself wishing the whole barrette scheme had never been suggested at all.

As it turned out, that return trip to the house, in which Alison held back tears in her red face and I sat speechless, staring out the window at the yellow divider line, was not indicative of our future as businesswomen. In fact, the popularity of the streamer barrettes only grew, and while I maintained steady sales with my bow pattern, soon Alison could hardly keep up with the demand for hers, for she had been persuaded by our parents to visit a second store, and the owner's substantial order had—or so it seemed to me in the moment—evened the score.

Later that month the owner of the first store, reconsidering her initial order and wanting to keep the barrette business all in the family, asked Alison to be the supplier of the streamer line. Was I glad of this, generous with my praise and proud? No: annoyed and jealous, forgetting all about the terrible expression on Alison's face when the woman in the first store had pushed her tray of barrettes to the side and ordered only mine. Even thinking about that morning, over twenty years ago, makes me feel guilty and ashamed. When the summer was over, so was our business. That fall, ribbon barrettes went out of style, to be replaced by something else—stickers or friendship pins—and I don't think either one of us ever made another pair.

I USED TO THINK I LIKED BEING THE OLDER ONE. I REALLY did, thought I loved being taller, faster, first, knowing things Alison did not and getting to decide whether I would tell them to her. We had a game I invented called the Six-Dollar game, which originated one day when I told Alison that if she could answer my trivia question, I would give her all the money I had at the time, which happened to be six dollar bills. Every time we played this game, up into our twenties, I asked only questions I would have bet my life she couldn't answer, questions to which I would not have known the answer myself if I had not just read about the subject in a *Scientific American* somebody had left at the dentist's office, never imagining its future role in an endless sibling ego match, one in which one person can't let the other catch up because then there would be no place for either to go. In all the years of the Six-Dollar game, long after inflation should have pushed the stakes higher, Alison never refused to play. And in all those years, never once did I ask her a question she would have a shot at knowing; to the contrary, I suggested a round only when I was in possession of a piece of trivia so obscure that occasionally I had forgotten its relevance. There are some questions not meant to be answered, and there is something to be said for being the person who, realizing the futility of the enterprise, keeps answering just the same.

An MIT professor named Frank Sulloway wrote a meticulously researched book on birth order and familial roles called *Born to Rebel*, and while I was dismayed to learn from it that I was unlikely to be able, as the older child, to break free from convention altogether and change the world in any meaningful way, I wasn't really surprised. For as long as I can remember, Alison has been the one who gave her dolls punk haircuts, colored outside the lines on purpose, laughed too loud in libraries, refused to wear socks even on the coldest snowy mornings, didn't speak when spoken to if she didn't feel like it, and stomped down the middle of the street as if she owned it, while I stood on the sidewalk chewing nervously on a cuticle and warning her that if she wasn't careful, she was going to get mowed down by a car. According to Sulloway, this disparity makes perfect sense. Firstborns tend to be "more jealous, anxious and neurotic" than their younger siblings, but also more "planful, assertive and likely to exhibit leadership." Accordingly, I have always considered myself tougher than Alison, more equipped in an emergency, less likely to panic: metaphorically able to take the wheel on an icy patch and steer the car over to the side of the road, ensuring our safety in spite of the adverse conditions. That I feel like this is largely a function of Alison herself, of how she sees me. In some ways I have become the person I see reflected in her eyes, never so much, though, as in her presence.

THE OLDER I GET, THE MORE I BELIEVE THAT SIBLING relationships inform every other relationship you will ever have—to such an extent, I think, that you can't even allow your mind to wander in that direction, in the same way you're not supposed to look at the sun. In the house we grew up in after the ages of six and seven, Alison and I had bedrooms next door to each other. Because my closet separated the two rooms, we didn't sleep on either side of a wall, and never engaged in the wall-knocking ritual my grandmother and I have in Martha's Vineyard, where each night ends with a pattern of raps initiated by one of us and returned by the other. Proximity for my sister and me bred mutual appreciation, sporadic contempt, but most of all a resigned dependence, made manifest in one case—during an extended bout of the flu—by an outdoor message line, on which a basket could travel from my bedroom window to hers, bearing notes, candy, stuffed bears on loan, and probably the occasional wad of chewed-up gum. This system didn't last long; it either fell apart, not to be restored, or was dismantled in the heat of an argument.

Most nights, after our father had descended the stairs while crooning "Goodnight Sweethearts," his personalized, pluralized version of the song that ended every episode of *Sha Na Na*, we just talked—so close in our little rooms that we didn't even have to raise our voices. On bad nights a talk would begin, innocuously enough, about, say, a project we were working on together for a contest at the library or about someone we both didn't like at ballet, and would turn into a vicious fight, at which point one of our parents would come upstairs to negotiate or, at the least, ask us to stop screaming at each other when there was company downstairs. On good nights the conversation would flow so easily that the wall between us seemed too thick and distancing, and I would sneak out of my bed and into Alison's closet, until, a bit later, a vicious, screaming fight ensued and I would either stomp or sulk back to my own room, grateful again for the distance between us.

Each August, however, we shared a bedroom, and for one halcyon month played at being the sisters we knew we could be if only we weren't related to each other and were more like the girls on *Facts of Life*, whose cheerful dorm room bore witness to countless girlish confidences and heart-to-heart discussions the likes of which Alison and I never had, in her closet or anywhere else. We also shared a dresser, and used the top drawer for our secret candy stash, as our mother tried to keep candy intake to a minimum and we were both fanatics for the stuff. We divided the window sill in our room in half, too, and arranged our art supplies on it, and having our colored pencils and embroidery floss and charcoal sticks so close together inspired us to share ownership, which we avoided doing at all costs at home. We stacked our library books on the little table between our beds, mine always the bed closer to the door, hers by the window, and on many nights read quietly before we fell asleep, soothed by each other's presence in the room.

Each of the twin beds in our Martha's Vineyard room had a reading light, whose controls could be accessed only by the person in the bed, and this led to periodic battles, as though we felt instinctively it would be a good idea to stay in practice for the coming autumn. Usually Alison would fall asleep and I would keep reading, sometimes until two or three in the morning. Most nights I simply turned off her light when she fell asleep, mine hours later when I started to see spots in front of my face. Sometimes I fell asleep before turning off either light, and my grandmother would tiptoe in and flick the switches, or I'd wake, bleary and confused just before dawn, and take care of it myself. Every once in a while, however, particularly if any animosity lingered from earlier that day, Alison would suddenly sit straight up in bed (always at the best part of whatever I was reading) and tell me I was keeping her up and had to turn off my light immediately. Now the fact that she had been asleep already for perhaps two hours never deterred her when she was in this mood, and the fact that I could easily have offered to read upstairs on the couch or on the stair landing, where I read during the day, never kept me from refusing to do so. A potentially flammable light war would follow, with Alison getting out of bed to turn off the wall switch, me getting up to turn it back on, both of us fueled by exhausting late-night fury. Eventually one of us would suggest some kind of a bribe or a deal, or I would stomp out with my book, pretending to concede while plotting my revenge for the following day.

I hated when Alison tried to make me stop reading in bed, and I hate it when my husband does so now, his unreasonable insistence on falling asleep in the dark provoking me so much that sometimes I persevere, holding my book up in defiance to catch any stray street light from the window—hard to come by on the sixteenth floor—when, again, I could easily go into the living room. What I really hated, although this was a one-sided, lower-pitched hatred, was Alison's snoring.

At home in Sudbury, with the wall between us, I couldn't hear her snore, even when it was winter and there was no racket from the legions of crickets surrounding our house. She would occasionally drop off in front of a television show or on her side of the back seat, but a sharp elbow to the rib cage or a hissed "Wake up" would usually put a stop to such pallid, early-stage snoring. Lying three feet away from me, however, separated only by our stacks of library books, she seemed to snore with a passion equal to, maybe even greater than that which fueled her waking self. Each inhalation led to a slow rumble, which crescendoed into a dull roar, which escalated to a bellow so hearty and sustained it seemed impossible she was actually asleep. At first I would keep reading, gritting my teeth, trying to focus on my own breathing and the words on the page. Every five minutes or so I would issue forth my hiss, so as not to wake our grandmother in the room next door, although considering the decibel of the snores, I probably could have afforded a regular shout. Then, when finally I'd had enough, I would resort to drastic measures.

The closet in our room was deep, and the back part was used for storage of various household necessities, including duct tape, always several rolls of it. With our sewing scissors, I would cut a four-inch strip, and in between the apex of a snore and the pause that initiated the next one, I would place the strip firmly across Alison's mouth. Once in a while, she would make a moaning sound or thrash around for a few seconds, but invariably the remedy worked like a charm. When I was finally done reading and ready to sleep, I would gently remove the tape from her face, ball it up and deposit it in the wastebasket, poking it under a magazine or soda can for extra measure. No one ever noticed it, and I congratulated myself on my ingenuity.

One night our mother poked her head in to check on us *after* I'd taped. Needless to say, she was horrified by the sight of Alison lying in bed like a kidnapping victim. I would like to point out, in my own defense, that during the entire period in which my mother made me remove the tape, throw out the rest of the rolls, and listen to a hushed yet pointed lecture on suffocation, Alison didn't so much as move a muscle. I did have the presence of mind to keep to myself my theory that I was actually acclimating her to sounder sleep patterns.

When Alison visits me now, she sleeps on my couch; it is rare these days that we share a room. It is entirely possible she has stopped snoring, or stopped snoring so enthusiastically; I now know that extra weight can contribute to this problem and interfere with a sound night's sleep in a number of ways. In fact, in her twenties, Alison was diagnosed with sleep apnea, an obesity-related condition that causes cessation of breath and can lead to fatality, and rushed to the emergency room in the middle of the night after an episode. But is it a stretch to think of us, in our twin beds on a bad snoring night, as a metaphor for the essential paradox of our relationship? In truth, I didn't want to take my book upstairs or move to my grandmother's bedroom each night for a number of reasons, but mostly because I loved sharing that room with Alison. For one reliable month each summer, I found an unnamed comfort in her beside me, the rise and fall of her chest as we breathed in and out from the same small patch of air. The strip of tape across her mouth let me have it both ways: I effectively silenced her, kept her from disturbing my reading, but if I reached out my arm and rolled just slightly onto my right side, I could gently touch her soft, flushed cheek.

T W O

food as fodder

Once my sister threw a knife at me. It was only a blunt dinner knife and probably would not have hurt me even if it had hit me, which it did not. It hit the glass I was holding and broke it into four or five pieces. The glass scattered, and a stain grew on the table. "Coke stains are really hard to get out," a cousin finally offered. No one else said a word. Somebody, probably my grandmother, picked up the pieces of glass, threw them away, and moved a serving dish to cover the spot. We finished dinner in a familiar, deliberate silence. I knew enough to let the incident die, pretend it had never happened, but I still think about it every so often. I brought it up a couple of months ago, and my family denied it had happened, even, especially, Alison. They didn't just not remember; they said it never happened, couldn't have happened, don't be ridiculous. I remember precisely where I was sitting at the table; I remember what triggered the throw. I had shot Alison a disparaging look for spreading extra butter on her roll; I had stared at her, eyebrows raised, while she took a bite. The next time I was at my grandmother's house, I looked in her cabinet. There were eight of the tall, thin amber glasses and only seven of the short fat ones.

LONG BEFORE WEIGHT WAS AN ISSUE IN OUR HOUSEHOLD, food was a focal point, in ways that still seem mostly good to me. Our friend Caroline, who was Alison's classmate, remembers coming over to our house to play with Alison after school one day. When Alison, rummaging exuberantly through the kitchen cabinets, asked if she wanted a snack, Caroline said sure. After a few fruitless minutes, Alison turned, resigned. "Well, there's nothing in here," she said, and I can imagine her resolute pout, a small stamp of her foot on the kitchen floor. "I guess we'll just have to go out to the backyard and dig up some potatoes." When Caroline told me this story years later, it took me a minute to realize why it struck her as funny. In my world it was only at other people's houses that snack food came in prewrapped packets or with prizes in the bags. Even at my grandparents' and aunts and uncles' houses we often picked fruit from the yard or baked something ourselves if we wanted something to eat. In our house, Alison had always been willing and able to whip up something delicious for the two of us to eat, regardless of what we had on hand.

It's funny: when people talk about weight problems, one of the first assumptions they make is that fat people eat bad food, that their eating habits were out of kilter from the start and got worse over time, that a really fat person can never understand what one *ought* to eat. In my experience, this is rarely true, and it was certainly not true in our house. I don't know of a single person, then or now, who provided more nutritious, well-balanced meals every day than our mother, and Alison grew up eating exactly what the rest of us ate. The rest of us were not fat. At my house, snacks were what today we call whole foods, as was almost everything in our refrigerator and kitchen cabinets. My mother had two major food rules, as far as I can recall: cereal could not list sugar as the first or second ingredient, and soda was bad for your teeth, although fine on special occasions. Sure, it was the 1970s, and we were served a few too many whole-wheat pita pockets and dried apricots for my taste, but unlike the parents of many of our friends, my mother never veered too far to the culinary left.

In fourth grade, for example, I made a friend who seemed to avoid having me over to her house; she always managed to end up at mine. Naturally this aroused my suspicion, and eventually I wrangled an invite, on a weekend no less, thanks to a scheduling snafu for a rehearsal of a play we both happened to be in. I asked for and was granted a tour, and, at first, I was puzzled. There was nothing weird about this girl's house, no erotic photographs on the living room walls, as was the case at a notorious classmate's, no bratty younger siblings, conspicuously ugly furniture, incontinent cats, nothing even slightly out of the ordinary. And then came lunch.

To her credit, my friend met her fate with dignity. She asked me to follow her into a room behind the kitchen I had correctly assumed was a pantry. The walls were lined with shelves, and the shelves were stacked, floor to ceiling, with boxes, bottles, and bags of food I had never heard of, all with the same generic labeling: bulgur, oat bran, sorghum, carob, and lots and lots of cans of beans. My friend's mother was waiting in the kitchen when we emerged with two cans of beans and something that vaguely resembled granola but was marked clearly, in all caps: SUGAR-FREE. My friend's mother, a greenish-pale slip of a woman with sunken eyes, smiled, and I saw in her eyes the gleam of the zealot. "If you girls eat all your bean casserole, you can have carob chips for dessert," she promised. My friend avoided my eyes.

After lunch, a dish so healthful and bland the Moosewood crew would have considered it penance, my friend suggested a bike ride. I was so eager to get away from her mother and the toxic smells in the kitchen that I was easy to persuade. Tottering on her brother's BMX, I followed her up to the town's main drag, to a tiny convenience store where, word had it, bad kids hung out, although on an early Saturday afternoon the parking lot was empty and only an old dog sat in the shade of the awning outside the door. "You want to buy or be lookout?" my friend asked, and I shrugged, confused, which she interpreted as a request for the lookout post. I assumed she was worried because we'd crossed Route 20, the town's big road, on bikes without permission and needed to avoid being spotted by our parents. A few minutes later she emerged, jumped on her bike, and rode wildfire into the woods behind the elementary school across the street from her house without a word to me. When I finally caught up, panting in exhaustion, she had spread the fruits of her labor on a tree stump: ten full-size candy bars, no two the same. I took my favorite and ate it in small bites the way I always did, coating first, then the caramel, as my scrawny bean-fed friend—and I do not exaggerate—consumed the remaining nine.

No, my mother was not a health-food freak, and it was not the lack of normal food that led me to abstain from so many foods for so many years and Alison to embrace a cornucopia of them. The tips my mother—who did all our shopping and cooking until she quit, quite literally, in the late 1980s, after showing my father how to use the microwave—took from the movement are the ones that have held over time, and although we didn't have junk food around the house, we were only subtly discouraged from coveting it. In fact, the way my mother cooked, and the way we ate, seems eerily prescient now as a model diet, with the sole exception—depending on your take on the protein gurus—of too much red meat, but in those days dinner was not complete, in many families, without a roast on the table or at least a hefty slab of beef in the center of each plate.

Each night until Alison and I were both in high school, we ate together as a family, often with one or more of our three grandparents, all of whom lived within five minutes of our house. With dinner we had salad, lettuce we grew ourselves in the enormous garden in the backyard along with some assortment of potatoes, sweet carrots, green and yellow beans, Swiss chard, peppers, summer squash, and various other rotating crops, depending partly on whether Alison and I had taken an interest during planting season. One year I grew little round watermelons, whose vines crept out of the garden's borders and over the lawn and which demanded a disproportionate amount of upkeep. But the garden was largely planned, planted, maintained, and sowed by our parents. Along with our father, we weeded when nagged, but the real work didn't interest us. What did interest us, as far back as I can remember, was what happened when the produce—and any other groceries—were brought indoors. If our mother's distaste for packaged foods had any effect on us, it was that, from early on, we both felt entirely at home in a kitchen.

My father did not possess my mother's innate sense of nutrition, but he also had very little to do with what any of us ate, which was for the best. His mother had struggled with her weight for much of her adult life and had been inordinately fond of fattening foods. He too had been on a number of diets over the years, although he tended to lose excess weight pretty quickly once he had gained it and is generally fit, more because of the hours of full court basketball he plays every day than as a result of healthy eating habits. When my mother was not around, he regressed to the overindulged child he'd been in Waterbury, Connecticut, in the 1950s. As soon as she left the house for parent-teacher conferences, or a PTA meeting, or (much more rarely) a dinner with friends, my dad would pile us into the car and drive to the grocery store in the center of town. There we would stock up on the makings of one of two meals: Kosher hot dogs, egg-enriched buns, sauerkraut, and potato chips, or thick-sliced corned beef, half-sour pickles, bulky rolls, and potato salad. You could practically see him at a formica table hunched over his plate, *Leave It to Beaver* on the living room television set, his mother replacing the hot dogs as he ate them and asking if he wanted more macaroni and cheese. It is to his credit that Alison and I have always held high standards for deli meats and have come to worship the hot dog as a vastly underrated player on the culinary stage. It is to my mother's credit that she pulled too large a share for so long when it came to household responsibilities, for otherwise we would be teeming with nitrates.

I STILL MAINTAIN, ALTHOUGH I AM WELL AWARE OF THE dark side, that people who appreciate good food are blessed. From humankind's earliest days, we have celebrated by sharing food, linking it inextricably to tradition,

culture, religion, family, community, joy. My family's celebrations, and there are many of them, are built around
food rituals shared by almost every member, and most of
us would not only notice but mourn their absence. We
were taught, from very early on, that what you eat and
how it is prepared can shape an experience. I cannot
imagine Easter without my grandmother's chocolate-
covered fondant eggs, a dark and luxurious handmade
precursor to the insipid Cadbury version, upon which
our names were written in cursive icing scrolls. Christmas
would not seem real or right without my mother's
Swedish smorgasbord, five separate courses served tradi-
tionally, beginning with cold seafood and leading up to a
white cake iced with pale green marzipan and a rice pud-
ding concealing an almond, the finder of which is supposed to be the next to be married and is inevitably
somebody under ten or in the midst of a divorce.

When I think of my immediate family members'
birthdays, the first association is our personalized cakes,
the kind of tradition my mother introduced effortlessly
and never let fail: raspberries and real whipped cream for
Alison; strawberries and whipped cream for me; chocolate, ganache, toasted almonds, and whipped cream for
my father; and varied inspirational attempts on the part
of Alison and me for our mother. In the old days it was
generally a lopsided yellow cake from *The Joy of Cooking*,
frosted in colors that only children will eat, such as blue. I
did not know whipped cream came in an aerosol can or a
plastic tub until I was a teenager. The only picture I have

ever seen of my first birthday is of me in front of my strawberry cake, which looks exactly the same as it did last year, when my mother drove it down from Massachusetts.

When my father's mother was alive, we had the traditional Jewish foods, too. One of our favorite rituals was having bagels at Bubby's on Sunday mornings, although in the 1970s these were hard to find in a legitimate version in our hometown. They were still, however, vastly superior to the frozen kind my father's sister was forced to buy in rural Vermont, and when we drove to visit Aunt Sheila, we usually had a bag of semiauthentic bagels between us in the back seat like a third half-Jewish child. Although my Bubby was notoriously secretive about her past, refusing to divulge exactly where or when she was born, no matter how hard I begged, food was one of the few subjects she would discuss without reservation. And like my mother's mother, she was a natural cook.

I still have an envelope on the back of which, at the age of eight or so, I wrote my Bubby and Aunt Lee's dueling kugel recipes, along with the words "They each say theirs is the best, not sure yet who is telling the truth." Bubby's roast chicken—which I realized years later she had brined, herself, in her tiny sink—was legendary, and every chicken I have ever roasted has aspired to its heights. I can never quite achieve its trifecta of succulent flavor, burnished, crispy skin, and meat so moist it's falling off the bone, and it is a great regret of mine (partly because the chicken was so good and partly because I never had the pleasure of cooking with her and wonder whether watching her would have opened some doors) that I never asked her how, exactly, she prepared it. Bubby died when I was fifteen, and I still make her kugel twice a year, and not just out of loyalty. My cousin Brook, who was only eight when Bubby died and now lives near me in New York, comes over to my apartment every month or so wearing Aunt Lee's camel's-hair coat and eats an awful lot of kugel if, by chance, I have prepared it. And though we rarely talk about Bubby during these meals, her presence—our blood connection—flavors every bite.

The truth is that it's the everyday meals of my childhood I remember most vividly, in particular those created in my Mormor's kitchen, centrally located between our house and my Aunt Sherry and Uncle Karl's on the other side of town. My mother's mother learned to cook from her mother, my great-grandmother, who came to this country from Sweden and worked in rich people's homes as a professional cook while raising seven children and maintaining her own house. My Mormor, like her mother before her, and my mother, too, is the kind of cook who eschews books and recipes except for pleasure reading and would blow away the competition on *Iron Chef* if she knew what it was and were not so modest about her culinary prowess that she would never agree to an appearance in the first place. At eighty-seven, she still lives and cooks in the house my mother grew up in. The thought of her preparing meals there—the image of a pot of soup on the wood stove and baking aromas emanating out to the porch and into the front yard—has taken on an urgency for me as the years go by. As long as she's cooking, I know she's still very much alive.

Recently, my father, my husband, and I moved a new stove into Mormor's kitchen, which retains its bones and warmth but has changed considerably since I was a kid. When we pulled out the old stove, we uncovered a narrow strip of the original carpeting along the wall. Our sense of smell is supposed to evoke the sharpest memories, but that scrap of orange and green, a pattern on which we used to shoot marbles, caused me to sink to my knees on the new white linoleum. While my father and Ben carried in the new stove and my grandmother sat watching from the bench on which five of us used to crowd when we were over for dinner, I leaned into a corner, regarding the room with the eyes of a ten-year-old.

Suddenly I remembered the cabinet drawer in which candy was hidden if you were lucky, the slightly musty air of the stairs to the cellar on which dry goods were stored, the coffee grinder that had been screwed to the wall near the refrigerator, the blueberry muffins we had made from the berries we'd picked just outside the front door, the cocktails my grandmother had made for us kids while the grown-ups drank real ones: an even mixture of orange juice and ginger ale. At a party a few months ago, I spotted a bottle of Schwepps and a pitcher of orange juice on the bar. As everyone around me sipped gin and tonic or cabernet, I closed my hand around a glass and shut my eyes, for a moment sitting out by my grandmother's pool reading *Little Women* for the tenth time and getting too much sun, while Alison built a vacation cottage for her bears under the massive pine tree my grandfather had planted in the middle of the yard.

It was my grandmother who prepared hundreds of meals for eight, twelve, or fifteen, so many nights after school, when my Uncle Karl tested me and my cousin Andy on our multiplication tables, and Alison and Jacy played Orphanage on the porch, with Brandon, always, as the resident dog. My grandfather, who died when I was thirteen, didn't cook much, but many of my memories of him are in that kitchen, too: requesting "five drops" of coffee, teaching me how to count in Swedish, showing me how to draw a portrait that looked like its subject and not just a generic face.

Every so often he did cook, usually when Alison and I were staying overnight at their house because our parents were away or out late in Boston, and when he cooked, he cooked only one thing: Swedish pancakes. He must have learned how to make them from his mother, although I realize now I don't know this for sure—another regret. I watched him as though through a microscope when he switched the roof on my mother's convertible from its hard top to the soft the summer before he died, even took notes on one of my countless yellow legal pads, not that I ever would have been entrusted with this particular job. But I took those pancakes for granted and have never attempted to make them myself. They were thin and creamy-yellow speckled with brown, and I ate mine rolled up with jam or just butter, as he did.

I THINK PALATES DEVELOP EARLY; I KNOW THAT PICKINESS does. During all of these family meals, different eating styles could be observed from the start. Andy, Jacy, and Alison all ate and, for the most part, ate what they were given. My cousin Brandon and I were finicky, eschewing almost all fruits and vegetables, most meats, sauces of any variety, and certainly any foodstuff not instantly recognizable to the naked eye. We liked our spaghetti with butter, our pizza plain, our bread white; and at the end of a meal, when Andy's, Jacy's, and Alison's plates were clean, ours looked as if a pack of only semihungry mice had descended, nibbled around the edges of the little piles, and retreated in defeat.

I wince thinking of the hours I spent, back in those days, picking little bits of food out of dishes. Peppers, onions, nuts, raisins, tomatoes, egg yolks, mushrooms, most meats except for bacon and chicken, all seafood, bread crusts, any cheese except for American, oranges, anything whole-grain or whole-wheat all made the walk of shame to the sides of my plate. I also didn't like different kinds of food to mix into each other—murky flavors—and any kind of gravy or sauce on top of the food was an immediate deal breaker. Until I was well over the customary age limit of twelve, I stuck to the kids' menus at restaurants, where I was virtually guaranteed to find some kind of noodles or chicken fingers or even a peanut butter and jelly sandwich.

On the other hand, Alison was always an omnivore, her palate sophisticated as soon as she graduated to solid foods. I was horrified by the things she not only ate but actually liked: avocados, which I considered green sludge; fish, the mere smell of which made me sick to my stomach; and, most dreaded of all, clams, which in my mind didn't even qualify as food—although, if I was desperate, I could be persuaded to sip at the creamy broth of a chowder while holding any mysterious rubbery chunks to the bottom of my mug with a spoon. (I did love the little hexagonal crackers.) One night, now firmly entrenched in our family mythology, company couldn't come for some reason or another, and my mother and Alison, who was about five at the time, polished off a giant pot of steamers, dipping them happily in broth and then butter, while I picked at a baked chicken leg, one of the few foods I would willingly eat.

There was a certain shallow pool under a bridge on Martha's Vineyard where my grandmother, mother, and Alison would look for mussels, which—when there were mussels to be found—always struck the three of them as very exciting, as though they were plucking nuggets of gold from the murky water instead of nasty, phlegmy creatures that didn't deserve the butter they were eventually bathed in.

"These are delicious," Alison would trill, dangling a particularly odious specimen from its black foot in front of my face as I turned away, protecting my pure bowl of noodles and trying not to look. Summers were especially hard for me, as the rest of my family thrived on the local fish markets. At dinnertime there would often be four plates set with stuffed clams, grilled salmon, mussels and dipping broth, and one plate bare but for a single hot dog, which I cooked in butter in a frying pan because nobody else did it precisely the way I liked.

Alison was not only a much more adventuresome eater than I was; she also had more of an appetite. We were both pretty active kids, with regular swimming lessons, ballet classes up to four times a week, after-school sports, a huge yard in which we spent hours a day, and cousins who preferred active games such as Whiffle ball and Four-Square, but even several hours of exercise rarely caused me to work up enough of an appetite to finish a meal. Unless she was sick, Alison almost always finished her meals, at home and at restaurants, where she advanced well before twelve to the adult menu and liked to suggest a variety of side dishes for the family to share. As I nibbled at the crust of a chicken finger, she'd explain to the rest of the table what she'd ordered, as my parents didn't necessarily know what celeriac was or why it was important to start many sauces with a French béchamel.

Whereas I ate the frosting off a cupcake, the middle of a sandwich, the white of a fried egg around its toxic yellow middle, Alison took her foods whole, as nature—or my mother—had intended, and would often have seconds. She also liked to snack. Because, as mentioned earlier, my mother did not believe in Twinkies or individual baggies of chips, creating innovative snack foods became one of our favorite shared after-school activities. With a careful delineation of roles, we could usually get through a cooking session without killing each other, although it was a batch of Snickerdoodle cookies run amok that led to my mother's firm rule of not taking calls from us at work unless blood was involved.

While I was not such a fan of eating, like Alison I always loved to cook, especially the snacks we made out of necessity. Many, if not most, of my friends were barely allowed in their own kitchens. Occasionally, if their mothers were in fantastic moods, we could make either Tollhouse cookies or cupcakes from a mix, but lots of my friends couldn't even break an egg without showering batter with shell bits, and none of our friends could conceive of the culinary escapades Alison and I shared in our kitchen, in which we were given free rein. Alison's instincts were always better than mine, and—my natural inclination to take control notwithstanding—I did acquiesce for the sake of the results, especially because for me it was more about the process and the aesthetics than the actual food.

One afternoon, during those first glory years when my mother went back to work full time and the house was our oyster, so to speak, we discovered a recipe for caramel

corn in one of the many cookbooks that were ours alone.
I could never get the proportions right, and I wasn't brave
enough to tinker, but Alison always knew if a little more
brown sugar or a little less butter would create a crisper
coating on the corn. Eventually a teaspoonful of molasses
added depth and perfected what soon became one of our
standbys. She doctored our basic chocolate chip cookie
recipe until the results were unrecognizable and vastly
superior, and to this day she won't tell me how. She
implicitly understood the fine points of deep frying, and
so we were able to attempt my great-grandmother's
doughnut recipe, a joyous feat that was, sadly, vetoed by
my mother, who was concerned about my propensity to
leave oil unattended on stovetops and what I have come
to think of as the baby-sitting incident of '83, during
which the Sudbury police department became more
involved in a particular pan of popcorn than I would have
necessarily desired.

Alison, always willing to modify or invent a recipe,
scoffed at my oppressive fear of failure. Like my mother,
who can make a mean marinade out of the remains of
five bottles on the bottom shelf of the refrigerator, Alison
is an inventor, a magician, an alchemist with food. It was
partly from her that I acquired my current devil-may-
care culinary style—to throw molasses and white sugar in
the bowl if there is no brown, to add extra vanilla to
baked goods, to brown a roux for just a second too long
for extra depth of flavor no matter what the recipe says.
When I was living in France during my junior year

abroad, I took a cooking class in the home of a chef in Montpellier, where I was studying (read: sunbathing and pretending to absorb the entire oeuvre of Marguerite Duras instead of just skimming for the racy parts). On the first session the chef explained that although she wasn't sure we Americans were sufficiently open-minded in the kitchen (can you feel the sneer on the page?), she was going to share with us a cooking secret that would improve every dish we ever made. Along with the other girls, I listened with bated breath, eager for the insider scoop that would transform even the lowliest American sandwich maker among us into a French gourmet.

"Always add a teaspoonful of salt to a sweet recipe and a teaspoonful of sugar to a savory one," she whispered, and as the other girls transcribed this morsel of wisdom in their *cahiers*, I sat back and rolled my eyes. Alison had figured that one out in first or second grade, when *savory*— spoken in the manner of an American actor imitating a French chef—was already one of her favorite words.

One Sunday morning at our grandparents' house, we decided to open a restaurant, not someday in the future when we'd left home and gone to culinary school, but that very morning, in time for brunch. Without telling a soul we made an enormous sign on a board that read *Papa's Pancakes*, the best name we could come up with under pressure, although my grandfather had been out in his machine shop working all morning and had no idea what we were up to. We brought the sign down to the end of the driveway and propped it up on the mailbox, then trotted back up to the house to make menus, pleased by our work and the anticipation of a few rollicking fights about who would be head chef and who would have to settle for waitress.

As we were setting the patio furniture with paper plates we'd smuggled out of the kitchen and ragtag linens from our dress-up box, a car pulled up the driveway and six strangers got out, looking around befuddled, as though they needed directions.

"Is this the pancake place?" the mother of the family asked, when I met her at the door, a premonitory knot forming in my stomach. For the next hour it was, and to their credit my mother and grandmother smiled benevolently at the guests, if not at us, as the family of six sat on the porch and ate pancakes, the only item available to them in spite of the elaborate menus.

WHEN ALISON WAS IN COLLEGE IN PROVIDENCE, OUR family discovered a restaurant there called Alforno, run by a husband-and-wife team of artists who had fallen in love with Italy and channeled their art into food. Whenever I was home from school, my parents and I would try to fit in the hour-long drive so we could eat there together. By this point I had become a more expansive eater, although I still tended to find something I liked and stick with it. I was also well on the way to my current modus operandi, which is to make a meal of as many small dishes as possible, three appetizers being preferable, for example, to a piece of meat and a mere two vegetable sides. I am what is called, in common parlance, commitment shy, especially when it comes to food.

My favorite thing to order at Alforno quickly became the antipasto, but as a main course, and if you have never tried the restaurant's particular version of what in the wrong hands can be a pallid pile of insipid cold cuts and tasteless chunks of flavor-leached carrot and cauliflower, I suggest you make room in your schedule for an excursion to Rhode Island. An Alforno antipasto consists of exquisite renditions of the following: grilled caponata, grilled peppers *agrodolce*, sautéed spinach and arugula, grilled onion, Tuscan bean purée, caramelized garlic, fresh mozzarella with cracked pepper, spiced olives, and a wedge of frittata, whose flavorings varied according to season. Although there were a few items I politely set on Alison's plate (the red peppers, for one), and I still brought half of each item home for the next day's consumption, this was one of the first meals I remember that made me see the possibilities of food as an art form and as much more than sustenance or part of a holiday tradition. Still, at the age of nineteen I would no sooner have prepared this array of dishes myself than I would have wolfed down a portobello, which always strikes me as a mushroom that has lived through a nuclear war.

When I graduated from college, my parents had a party for me in Sudbury in the backyard of their house, a cookout, to which all of my relatives and many friends were invited. We grilled sausages and vegetables, Mormor brought paprika-dusted deviled eggs, my Aunt Linnea brought beautiful loaves of homemade bread, my Aunt Sherry brought her famous apple pies, and Alison whipped up a big salad and some kind of a cake. I was so dazed in the anticlimactic fog of the beginning of the rest of my life that other than the food, I don't remember a single thing about this event—not opening gifts of fancy pens, or showing off my very first suit, for so-far-theoretical job interviews, or passing around my diploma to people who had to feign interest while fully aware it would soon end up in the basement. The next morning, when I woke up in a state of low-grade panic, Alison announced she would be making dinner for us that night, in honor of my graduation, just for immediate family and Mormor. That night we gathered around the big coffee table in my parents' living room and sat on the couches on either side of it, waiting for Alison, who was engaged in solitary vocal and apparently stressful last-minute preparations in the open kitchen, just out of view. When she set down an enormous platter in front of me, we were all silent, until finally Alison spoke.

"If nobody appreciates this, I'm taking it away," she snarled, her voice in stark contrast to her palpable nervousness. It was the Alforno antipasto, of course, recreated meticulously, each dish in the same position the restaurant placed it, each component a virtual twin to Alforno's version, glistening with olive oil and twinkling with shavings of sea salt. A closer look, however, revealed that Alison had tweaked the recipes ever so slightly, eliminating the red peppers she knew I hated, modifying the fritata filling to my specific taste.

How did I come to love food? How on earth did I transform myself from a child who would not eat a sandwich if it had a leaf of lettuce in it into a person who spends more time thinking about and preparing food in all its varied guises than is probably totally healthy or sane? There are many reasons, including the fact that I am a member of a family who loves to eat and I was bound to come around some time or another; that my grandmother, mother, and aunts were such excellent, effortless cooks; that from a very early age I was not just allowed but encouraged to cook. But those cannot be the only reasons.

My cousin Brandon still subsists primarily on pizza, lasagna, and beer (which replaced Coke as the beverage of choice in his twenties), and with the exception of my cousins Inga and Ellen, out of the nine of us, only Alison and I truly love cooking as of yet. I think the x factor is Alison, who long before she went to art school and became a professional cook herself, saw the powerful connections between food and design, cooking and creativity, a generous heart and a generous table. I think that her innate open-mindedness and the immense pleasure she took in trying new foods and in cooking with new ingredients rubbed off on me over the years. And fortunately I have always been able to see—and keep—food and weight in two separate categories, even as I know this is not possible for most people, and is certainly not true for my sister.

UNTIL NOW, I HAVE PAINTED A PRETTY ROSY PICTURE of my family's relationship to food. Like all pictures, however, this one reflects only one angle of the story. That is not to say it is untrue—it is merely the red, glossy side of the apple and not the one with the gnarled skin and the bruise. I actually don't remember when I first became aware that Alison was not eating just to get full, and one reason I don't remember is that Alison kept her binge eating to herself. When we sat around the dining room table or on the high stools at the kitchen counter, she never consumed an exorbitant amount of food, although she often added butter to dishes I didn't think needed more. I think her public eating habits were designed to conceal any eating she did in private, which turned out to be quite a bit. It was not until high school that I found empty cookie boxes and scrunched-up bags of chips in the bottom of the garbage can in the bathroom, or that I spotted a telling corner of neon packaging peeping from under her bed. It was then—when I became aware of the effort involved in concealing these binges—that I realized the problem wasn't going to go away on its own. Bingeing is a common precursor to obesity. According to the National Institutes of Health, up to four million Americans are binge eaters, who compulsively consume vast amounts of food at one sitting. In 2003, researchers in Switzerland discovered that a mutation of the melanocortin 4 receptor causes binge eating—it was not a lack of willpower that was making Alison stuff herself in secrecy—and leads so many to the top of this slippery slope.

When Alison started, slowly, to gain weight at about the age of ten or eleven, my parents subtly dissuaded her from overeating, so subtly from my perspective that sometimes I didn't even clue in, although she became sensitive to even the slightest pressure almost as soon as it started. I can remember a few times when one of them took me out for an ice cream when it was just the two of us on an errand, after claiming, in front of Alison, that we didn't have time. I don't think any of us anticipated how much weight Alison was going to gain, however. I know I always assumed she was just going through a chubby phase—how I have always hated that *c* word—and would one day weigh around what I weighed, with minor adjustments for height. At first, in fact, her weight gain was a mild distraction on the family radar screen, detectable only by an occasional cleared throat, the pushing of apples as after-school snacks, sporadic outbursts of "stop watching me eat."

Getting fat doesn't happen overnight. As an observer of the process, however, I can testify that the pounds creep up so slowly that the weight gain seems to have occurred without anyone noticing. It's like looking into a camera at a scene that appears out of focus, and twisting the mechanism a millimeter to the right and then to the left and then back—until suddenly the blur becomes perfectly crisp and the image appears. I can picture Alison as an average-size fifth grader and an obese eighteen-year-old, and practically nothing in between—the in-between years remain out of focus, for the most part, even now, even when I strain to remember them. I can picture her on a family trip to Bermuda just after her most successful diet, probably because we have a photograph of her wearing her favorite white denim jacket and her beloved Silver City Pink lipstick, which I disparaged as overly dramatic and too "L.A." but secretly coveted and occasionally tried on for the sole benefit of the bathroom mirror. In this photo she is posing, and pouting a little, although the corners of her mouth are turned up in a sleepy half smile; and maybe it's just the powers of hindsight, but to me she looks good, if a little uncomfortable, as though she'd woken up, Freaky Friday–style, in someone else's body. It disturbs me to think that during the years Alison gained all that weight, until she was clinically obese and trying to lose weight, I was barely aware that she was silently struggling. When she had reached what was to be her maximum weight, it was really too late to pitch in with concern; it was time to start thinking about how I might have contributed to the problem.

Growing up, I was often asked why Alison didn't just go on a diet. I had certainly suggested dieting to Alison, and offered plenty of constructive criticism when she was on one, but when I was handed this question, I instantly bristled and snapped. There should be a commandment or a constitutional amendment against criticizing somebody's immediate family to his or her face. I actually think I may have asked a few people offering secondhand diet advice why they didn't go to finishing school to learn some manners, which tended to shut them up pretty quickly, but Alison kept gaining weight and people kept giving *me* tips, usually in what they seemed to believe was a helpful way. When I was really at my wits' end, or confronted by a repeat offender, I would nod thoughtfully as the suggestion was made, then feign terrific enthusiasm— which, as anyone who knows me can testify, is a bad sign.

"What a wonderful idea," I gushed to more than one advice giver. "I don't know why we didn't come up with that one on our own! It *would* make all the difference if she could just cut back on sweets."

In my twenties, when you might assume my peers would know better, people continued to give me advice intended for Alison, as though I were her nutritionist and personal trainer rolled into one confrontational package, as though their singular words of wisdom could possibly counteract a decade of compulsive eating. After a while I just gave up. When a new friend or acquaintance would begin, "You know what just might work for your sister?" I would pretend I was my cousin Ellen, who once told me that one of the benefits of being profoundly deaf and wearing hearing aids was the ability to remove them and smile in bliss as you were talked at by someone you had no desire to listen to. I have almost mastered this sleight of ear, although occasionally I am caught when I tune back in just as the term *Pritikin* or *spinning class* is being uttered with utmost sincerity, and I blink in dismay for an instant too long.

Are there areas other than weight loss in which people who are otherwise sensible and polite feel free to toss out their ideas to improve you? I had a great-aunt who liked to assess your hairstyle to your face and compare it to previous incarnations, but we all accepted this as bad manners not worth getting up in arms about and rolled our eyes at each other over her head. I understand that people are interested in weight, anxious for any insight, however obtained, as to how to keep from gaining it, eager to help prevent others from a fate worse than death. That is why the weight-loss market in this country is vast and continually expanding—it is built on a shaky foundation of false hope and shadowy motivation. I understand, too, that people are uncomfortable talking about weight, unless it is in the context of losing or lost— we constantly ask each other, "Have you lost weight? What's your secret?" and "How do you ever manage to stay so thin?" These lines, uttered to a friend or a colleague with a touch of envy, inevitably result in the recipient's glowing satisfaction, the speaker's silent pledge to give up carbs or get back to the gym. We never talk about weight gain, unless it's hypothetical or in the form of gossip, in the hushed tones people probably used in discussing polio or leprosy when these illnesses were cultural fears.

OF COURSE ALISON WENT ON DIETS; HOW COULD SHE
not? Starting at about the age of thirteen, she went on
plenty, some traditional, others more obscure, all doomed
to ultimate failure, as most diets seem to be. Throughout
her teenage years, in fact, she was, at least theoretically,
on a diet more often than not. Although I was certainly
aware she was devoting a lot of time and energy to what
she was eating, I was a teenager, too, and the picayune
details of my own existence—precalculus, Lacrosse try-
outs, the perfect scrap of material with which to patch
my jeans—consumed so much of my own energy that
there was little left over for empathy. In fact, as Alison
likes to point out, I did more damage than good by criticizing her efforts and slip-ups, motivated both by genuine
concern and the image of the perfect little sister whose
clothes I could borrow, who always stood tantalizingly
just out of reach.

    She refused to talk about her diets with me, and I
never knew how much she weighed. I rarely tried to initi-
ate a discussion about one of her diets, but I did feel
frustration rise on those rare occasions when she ate
mindlessly and compulsively in my presence, such as in
front of the television or riding somewhere in the car. I
remember the powerful urge to grab a bag of French fries
from her and throw it out the window. As much as I was
aware on some level that she couldn't control the way she
was eating, I was still shocked when I saw her behavior up

close. It was clear that the eating was not about actual hunger—in fact, sometimes it made me queasy to imagine such a large amount of greasy food in my own stomach—my revulsion and urge to save her from herself was a visceral reaction.

At about the age of ten I developed a tic, a tilt of my head to one side with a concomitant rolling of my eyes. Throughout my childhood and adolescence it—and its subsequent variations—was confined primarily to our house. Alison, of course, soon became an avid scout of these tics, increasing her attention to them in direct proportion to mine of her eating patterns. When she would spot me looking upset as she scraped the bottom of a bowl of ice cream, she would imitate my tic, which I called a "twitch," rolling her head around in a exaggerated version. After a few years of such back-and-forth meanness, the criticism and scrutiny began to cancel each other out, unless one of us was feeling particularly persecuted or retaliatory, in which case lashing out remained a surefire hit. In my twenties, when my father and I were both diagnosed with obsessive-compulsive behaviors and—in my case—mild Tourettic tics (which have since faded), I still did not make a link between my own compulsions and Alison's compulsive eating. It was not until after her surgery that she pointed out what now seems an obvious link: compulsive behaviors are flip sides of the same coin, a vein that runs through our family like copper through ore.

Most of the time when Alison wolfed down food, I made little comments or gave disapproving looks from across the table. I knew full well that a constant influx of pointed stares and caloric statistics was not going to make Alison stop eating. I knew so for a number of reasons, primarily that when I saw someone else acting the way I did, I felt rage and disgust—how dare that idiot judge my sister or even dare to imagine doing better in her place! I also saw that being judged or disproved of made Alison justifiably angry and defensive, as it would any thinking person with a sensitive bone in her body, as it made me when she drew attention to the head tilt that I knew, on some level, I could not control. Sometimes, when a waiter expressed barely detectable surprise at her order, or a salesgirl eyed her skeptically as she browsed through clothes that were probably too small, I thought I could catch a fleeting sense of Alison's anger and defensiveness. It made me wonder: if I was so furious on Alison's behalf that I was seething and shaking, then how angry must Alison have been for—and at—herself? In such moments I had insight into Alison's locked bedroom door. If you are a compulsive eater, hungrier than you are meant to be by virtue of your biology, unable to lose weight by methods most people are not strong enough to undertake, seclusion makes a comfortable restaurant.

And sometimes I did know just how angry she was. Long before Alison had a weight problem, she could have taught an assertiveness class, a class that I should have been signed up for, although I managed to learn a few tricks from the master over the years. In a certain frame of mind—and depending on whom she was with at the

THE WEIGHT OF IT   73

time—Alison would tell off the person who was disparaging her, or would make her feelings known, sometimes so effectively that my natural inclination was to stand up and cheer. One night at a Chinese restaurant in our town, the waiter led my family and some friends to a large round table in the back of the main room. Before any of us had chosen a seat, he bowed slightly and pulled out the chair in the corner away from the kitchen with a flourish and gestured at Alison.

"I think this lady will be most comfortable here," he said. I was standing next to Alison and had heard every word; the rest of our party were removing their coats, arranging who wanted to sit by whom and chattering among themselves. Alison gave the waiter a cold, steely glare. Her mouth opened, then closed, and she turned in an elegant pivot and walked straight through the room and out the front door.

"Where's she going?" my father asked me, with a shrug of confusion. I walked over to him and my mom and told them what the waiter had said.

"I'm sure she misunderstood," one of them said.

"I'm sure she did not," I countered. That night the restaurant lost out on a hungry party of eight.

There were other such incidents, in clothing stores and restaurants, at holiday celebrations and family gatherings, and always the rest of us were slightly exasperated, wished Alison could just let it go. And I'm sure there were also occasions when Alison *did* misunderstand a look or a phrase, assumed the worst of an innocent bystander or even a kindhearted soul. She was and remains paranoid that people are looking at her or talking about her, always in a negative way. But really, how could she not be? Today, when I notice a family member rolling his or her eyes in that "there she goes again" kind of way I know so well because I helped invent it, I try to remember how it evolved, in a harsh reality where paranoia was possibly the only reasonable stance.

Obesity colors every aspect of a person's life—physical, social, and emotional—but it is especially devastating for the very young. In 2003 the University of California at San Diego published a study in the *Journal of the American Medical Association* that determined that the quality of life for obese children or teenagers is "roughly equivalent to that of pediatric cancer patients." Even more so than cancer, obesity is a condition that cannot be concealed or dealt with privately. It is a public disease with a public face, and its sufferers confront their critics every time they leave their homes. While most obese teenagers are not clinically depressed, they almost always report feeling socially isolated, which is not surprising; for Alison the sense of isolation was most frequently manifested as anger, even rage. And the problem is only getting worse: in the 1960s, 7 percent of children in this country met the definition for obesity; in the late 1990s, the figure had jumped to 15 percent.

If you watch television or read the newspaper, you are familiar with the constant speculation as to why Americans—and in particular American children—are getting fatter so fast. Most people assume the trend is due to poor eating habits; too many hours spent watching television, playing video games, and surfing online, and lack of exercise, in school and otherwise. While these factors play a role in the rapid rise of childhood obesity, they seem to point a blaming finger at parents and children alike and to ignore the root cause affected by these environmental factors: biology—more specifically, according to researchers at the Medical College of Georgia, a mutation in a receptor for the hormone leptin, which signals to appetite control centers in the brain that sufficient fat has been stored. As regards these studies, Dr. Jeffrey Friedman of the Howard Hughes Medical Institute at Rockefeller University writes: "All of the genes that are currently in the population, they aren't any different from the genes we had 100 years ago. It is the environment that has changed and that is causing this genetic susceptibility to come out. In trying to lose weight, the obese are fighting . . . a battle against biology, a battle that only the intrepid take on, and one in which only a few prevail." No wonder Alison was often so angry; it is hard enough to grow up without the added stress of taking on your body every day, knowing, on some level, whether or not you can acknowledge it to yourself, that you are destined to lose.

HOW DID ALISON GO FROM A HEALTHY, ACTIVE TEN-year-old to a plump eleven-year-old to an overweight

eighth grader to obese at fifteen? Although I've certainly
spent a lot of time thinking about it, I'm still not entirely
sure. There is no question that genetics was not in her
favor. Regardless of our strong resemblance to each other
as children, in very early photographs of the two of us
you can see the subtle differences in our bodies, tem-
plates of what was to come. Her love for food—its colors,
tastes, and shapes—the buying, preparing, and eating of
it, I think, was a factor as well. But mainly, I think, she was
born with a biological imperative to gain weight.

Growing up, I always sensed that Alison lacked whatever it was that made me get full. Long after I'd set down
a bag of chips, she'd keep on eating, almost robotically, as
though the only way she could stop was if the bag was
forcibly removed from her hand. If options were offered
for food or drink—a large or a small—she chose the large,
without stopping to think if she actually wanted that
much of whatever it was. These habits did not seem
alarming to me when we were children, and I don't
think—at first, anyway—they did to anyone else. Pediatri-
cians, child-rearing experts and parenting guides have
long stressed the dangers of creating weight hang-ups in
children, citing a link to lifelong eating disorders, self-
esteem problems, and even depression. However, recent
studies indicate that the pattern of Alison's weight gain
was predictable, its outcome doomed from the start. The
New England Journal of Medicine reported in 1997 that
"more than 50% of obese children over the age of 6 will

continue to be obese into adulthood, and 70 to 80% of obese teenagers will remain obese as adults."

It is too simple to say that size is destiny, and it is ludicrous to pretend that environment and emotional factors play no role in weight gain and obesity. But it is dangerous and counterproductive and flat-out inaccurate to ignore biology's starring role in this cast, not just as a determining factor but as an exacerbating one. For once Alison started to put on the weight she had been programmed to gain, it must have pretty quickly become next to impossible to see her way out.

THREE

coverings

According to legend, Gertrude Stein posed for Pablo
Picasso almost a hundred times between 1905 and 1906.
Uncharacteristically, Picasso experienced great frustration with the portrait and kept painting over his notorious subject's face in thick, blotting brush strokes. Finally,
in the spring of 1906, he turned to Stein and asked her
to leave. He announced that he intended to paint her distinctive features—her very expression—from memory,
once she was far from his studio. "Why?" she must have
asked, puzzled by the master's visible agony, but by
then Picasso had found words for his predicament. He
explained to Stein, who probably understood all too well
what he meant once she'd had time to mull it over with

Alice B. Toklas or a young, eager Hemingway: "I can't see you any longer when I look."

I would take Picasso's statement one step further. I think that once we reach adulthood, most of us can't see our own bodies anymore for too much looking, on our own part and by the rest of the world. In college I took an early-childhood education class that required several hours of observation each week in the nursery school on campus. The work entailed bringing a clipboard into a long narrow room behind one of the main classrooms and taking notes on a selected child you scrutinized through a soundproof, one-way window, which appeared to the children as an enormous mirror. Before the first session, most of us whined about the assignment, tried to get out of it. The secret observation was pointless; we knew these kids and were certain they wouldn't behave any differently from the way they did while we were around. It was creepy; there was a voyeuristic quality to the exercise that seemed to defy the tenets of our open, liberal education. And finally, it was early. (Like many college students, I had finessed a schedule that enabled me not to be much of anywhere before noon any day of the week. Nursery school started at 7:00 a.m.) But our professor insisted, and early one morning I sat in the narrow watch space with two sweating Diet Cokes, doodling on my clipboard and waiting for the kids to arrive for free play. My subject was named Tristan, and I had chosen him expressly because he was an easygoing, well-adjusted, intelligent child who seemed unlikely to demand much of me in the way of obscure child development theories or even any real observing.

When Tristan and his classmates filed into the room, they headed immediately for the big rug in front of the mirror. Many of the kids were so close we could have reached out and touched them if not for the window. I looked on, idly, as a notoriously difficult twosome broke out into a fight over Legos on the far corner of the rug; but after a minute or two, I became transfixed by Tristan, in spite of myself. Like six or seven other kids, he had pulled himself so close to the mirror that he was touching it. At first he sat with his legs straight out, his feet pressed against their mirror images. Then he bent his knees and edged closer, then closer still, until his forehead was pressed into the mirror, his body folded over his bended knees. His hands were on the glass, too, although he kept using them to push himself back, so as to get a close-up view and then one with a little more distance. For a full twenty minutes, Tristan sat entranced by himself, changing his pose so as to get a better look at his torso, legs, and face, but his eyes never left the mirror. At several points I became convinced he could see us, was actually a subversive genius toying with us, trying to teach us a lesson. The only problem with this theory was that the majority of the kids in the class spent most of their playtime engaged with their own unwavering gaze.

Later that afternoon I was at the library checking out some novels. I had been thinking about those kids all day, how when faced with willing peers, enthusiastic teachers, and a room full of toys, they had chosen to eschew all external stimulation and study themselves. With herculean effort befitting the laziest of undergraduates on a virgin excursion, I managed to find several books on child development and a free table. As it turned out, two-year-olds are often narcissistic, fascinated by bodies and faces they are only just getting to know. Although I know plenty of adults who are consumed by their bodies and faces— spending thousands of dollars and hundreds of hours a year on exercise, clothing and cosmetics, and customized diets—it is arguable that most don't actually see the bodies and faces they are trying to "fix." Rather, as teenagers, we gradually lose sight of the physical selves we admired in mirrors as toddlers, appreciated for their strength and agility, and used with abandon. By the time we are adults, we have grown to dislike or distrust our physical selves. When we look in mirrors, we see only flaws: the teeth never quite straightened by braces, the skin beginning to show signs of age, the too high forehead inherited from a parent we've never quite forgiven for the indignity.

I AM NOT ONE OF THOSE PEOPLE WHO BUY THE "FAT IS fabulous" movement or think "fat is just a state of mind." I don't believe that fatness is primarily an emotional problem, or even that people are fat because of emotional problems, although of course both of these are sometimes true. I don't believe, ever, that anyone likes to or deserves to be fat. To be fat is to be ignored, made fun of, scoffed at, disparaged, joked about, condescended to, mocked, and belittled—not every minute of every day, not unequivocally, not by every person, but often enough, by enough people, and in enough situations that it takes a toll on the person's very soul, a fragile construct in the strongest of us. A 2002 study in the journal *Health Economics* reported that people more than thirty pounds overweight are paid less than peers for the same work; across the board, obese people face discrimination on a par with, if not worse than, that based on gender or race. I'm not sure why we are so afraid of and hateful to fat people. I suspect our feelings come largely from a "there but for the grace of God" mentality, anxiety simmering just below the surface that at any moment our own weight could slip irrevocably beyond our control. The average American woman, in fact, is 5 feet, 4 inches and 140 pounds. According to a recent report from the *Journal of the American Medical Association*, 64.5 percent of us are overweight, and 31 percent—*sixty million people*—are clinically, morbidly obese.

It is not just our shoddy treatment of fat people that makes it better, by far, to be thin. It is true that there are unhealthy thin people, existing on champagne and cigarettes, or lettuce and saltines, and there are fat people who exercise daily, eat well-balanced meals full of vitamins and minerals, and have healthy cholesterol levels and acceptable blood pressure. However, fat people die earlier and more regularly from heart disease, strokes, cancer, and diabetes. A 2003 study by the American Cancer Society reported that 14 percent of all cancer deaths in men and 20 percent of cancer deaths in women may be attributed to obesity. In fact, fat people die earlier than thin people, period. Low body weight is one of the most reliable indicators of longevity, regardless of other factors such as nutrition and level of physical activity.

Being fat turns many ordinary activities or situations into a struggle. If you are obese, you will find many seats, such as those on airplanes and in movie theaters, too small to accommodate your body. You will find it a challenge to buy comfortable, good-looking clothing. You will realize that many recreational activities seem designed to make you feel or look uncomfortable: sunbathing, shopping, almost all competitive sports. Your body will ache with the weight of itself if you stand for too long, or walk too far, and it is inevitable that at some point you will experience health problems due solely to your size. Your heart will bear too great a burden, as will your back and your legs. Your breathing will become irregular when you sleep, or stop altogether, cutting off blood flow to your brain. Your arteries will clog, insulin levels will fluctuate, heart will pound when you walk too far or too fast. Whenever I stumble upon an article by or an interview with an obese person who claims to be one hundred percent content with her weight, I cannot stave off the first words that come to my mind: that is a lie. A few months after her surgery, Alison told me she finally knew she was really losing weight when for the first time in fifteen years she could look down and see her own feet. If that doesn't knock you for a loop, I'm not sure what will—maybe the fact that a year later she called to tell me she had just crossed one leg over the other while sitting in a chair.

I am not asserting that thin people are better than fat people, just better off on the whole. I am not indicting fat people, or pitying them, and I hope that this point goes without saying, but I have my doubts that it will. There is a politically correct school of thinking that is always claiming decent people to be free from fat prejudice, fat people to be "differently sized" but otherwise just like the rest of us. There are also lots of people, and not just in the film industry, who would prefer never having to look at a fat person for the rest of their lives. Some of my own friends have made strikingly insensitive comments about Alison, although they would be horrified to have this pointed out to them. One friend told me that she thought Alison would be much happier if she would just accept being fat and stop yearning to be thin. This, I imagine, would be akin to accepting a constant, terrible headache and giving up wishing it would go away. It also strikes me as unbelievably hypocritical: How can you not want for other people what you want for yourself, have been blessed with by the happy accident of your birth?

If you grow up with obesity—your own or a loved one's—you don't need the map of the human genome to know that there is a genetic component. When I visited the genome exhibit at the Museum of Natural History in New York a few years back, however, I was surprised to see the genome for obesity marked on a wall-size display, along with the markers for its hapless cousins: the *tendency* to be overweight and even the *tendency* to be *slightly* overweight. As it turns out, even minute gradations in size are predestined at birth.

As I contemplated the partially mapped out genome on the wall, I thought about the bodies of the people I knew well, especially those I had known over long periods of time. My father, a classic yo-yo dieter, has been both very overweight and almost dangerously thin, but most of the time he is medium size, regardless of fluctuations in diet and exercise. An acquaintance of mine is naturally big boned and solid and was when I first met her, but over a period of years she regulated her caloric intake so aggressively that it never veered by a digit, and she began exercising for hours each day, seven days a week, whittling herself down to just about average for her height. When I imagine the immense strain and mental energy it must take to maintain her unnatural, slightly smaller shape, it makes me tired and sad, although some people get through their lives by such regimens. I guess I'll be the first to admit that it's not fair to criticize what you don't understand.

WHEN ALISON AND I WERE VERY YOUNG, WE WERE BOTH tiny and—like our mother at our ages—always the smallest children in our grades. When you are little in elementary school, your size becomes a part of your per-

THE WEIGHT OF IT 87

sona: you are the top of the pyramid, the first or last in line, the mascot of popular older girls, who like to mock-maternally fetishize kids in lower grades, and sometimes even the star of the play—based not on talent but on your bankable cuteness. At the time we reveled in this, felt sorry for the girls in our class who were lanky and tall, or medium size and therefore lost in the crowd.

When we were children, I had a lot of opportunity to contemplate both Alison's body and mine, although neither was of particular interest to me until much later on. When I took ballet classes in high school, in a dance studio positioned on campus so everybody entering or exiting the gym had a long view into the windows lining the barre, I thought so much about how I looked that I had trouble focusing on the instruction. All I could think about was whether my new white leotard was unflattering or if the boys on their way to soccer practice were looking at me or the girl in front of me and whether they could tell I was checking them out through the window, because I'd just smacked into the wall. As a child, when I spent several hours a day in a ballet studio for a number of years, I never thought about my appearance, or that of the other girls in my class. I coveted one girl's extension, another's glittery leg warmers, but I never compared my body to theirs, only our talent and styles. I remember when I was fourteen and about to give up ballet because I had decided I wasn't going to pursue it as a profession, the owner of the ballet school sighed a small sigh of relief.

"I'm glad," she said. "You're very good, but I'm afraid you'll be much too short for a corps de ballet." Shell-shocked, since she had always encouraged me, I asked if she thought any of the seven other girls in my section would make it, and she chose the last girl I would have expected. "Melissa, I suspect," she predicted, correctly, as it turned out. "Her body is perfect."

Until we were well into adolescence, Alison and I and our cousins spent most summer days at my grandparents' swimming pool. For three months each year we lived in our bathing suits, would pull on shorts and sandals if required by law but were always annoyed by the inconvenience. Sometimes I wonder if Alison started comparing herself early on to the rest of us, all knock-kneed and hollow chested, so thin as children you could count our ribs just from looking. I actually remember doing so a couple of times with one of my cousins, but counting each other's ribs was an endeavor in which Alison would not have been able to participate; even as a small child she never had bones that showed through her skin.

Although Alison was not notably overweight until high school, she herself was far more aware of her size and how it differed, if ever so slightly, from that of her peers. In sixth grade, when I recall her being only slightly larger than I was, she used to have one of her best friends sit on her stomach in an attempt to flatten it when they were hanging out after school and watching *General Hospital*, forbidden fruit in our house, which Alison was sufficiently bold to pluck and enjoy. Sometimes they would run around the house for exercise, through the rooms on the first floor, which at best made an awkward, potentially hazardous track. I don't know if these early forays into alternative weight-loss techniques were her idea or her friend's, but I wonder if it was around this time, too, that Alison became sensitive to the insecurities of girls around her, universally uncomfortable in their changing bodies and anxious about what the ideal was supposed to look like.

According to Alison, it was also at this age that an outsider first commented on her weight. We had been asked by our mother's cousin Ellen, whom we had always idolized, to be junior bridesmaids in her wedding, and my mother took us to a tailor to have us measured for our beautiful rose-colored dresses. I felt like a princess looking at the sketches of the dress, which reminded me of the costume I had worn as Clara in the *Nutcracker* and coveted so intensely that the costume mistress half suspected I would try to take it home with me when the production came to an end. When we arrived at the tailor's, I was hopping up and down with excitement, and offered to go first to be measured, a process that turned out to involve standing still for an uncomfortably long time and having pins jabbed into me while Alison smirked. Finally my turn was done, and I settled on a chair with my book. When it was time to leave, we headed to the car, and I couldn't help but notice that Alison seemed annoyed by something, not enraged, but definitely square on the side of upset. It came out that while winding pink silk around her body and surveying the pattern, the dress-maker had told my mother she would need additional fabric to complete Alison's dress.

I DON'T REMEMBER HOW OLD ALISON AND I WERE WHEN the difference in our weight became noticeable to other people, an issue in our family. It was a slow creep, but I think the fact that I was a scrawny kid may have made the contrast between us greater than it would have been otherwise, because when I look at pictures now, up until seventh or eighth grade the difference is very subtle: Alison looks slightly softer around the edges than I do, smooth curves instead of bony angles. In fact, it was only because of our Bubby, my father's mother, that I had any concept of fat as the opposite of thin and as a negative factor at all.

I knew that Bubby was fat, partly because people always said so when they spoke about her. It's funny now, seventeen years after her death, that when I look at pictures of her even at her heaviest, she doesn't look that fat to me. Of course the world has changed, grown fatter since her death, so maybe it's my perspective that has shifted. When Bubby moved nearby and we were still in elementary school, my father used to take her to her regular Weight Watcher meetings, because she had never learned to drive. In the summer we liked to go along for the ride, because my dad would take us to Friendly's for ice cream cones while we were waiting for her. Never did

I link the two in my mind—that my grandmother was at a meeting to track the weight she was struggling desperately to lose, while we indulged in cones up the street: coffee ice cream for my dad, lemon sherbet for me, and bubble gum, or another novelty flavor, for Alison, who remains more apt than either of us to try something new. I can't remember what else we did during these meetings. I don't even recall the location, although it must have been a church (which Bubby would have hated) or some other building in close proximity to Friendly's, and I don't remember waiting in the car or running errands during the meeting. In my mind, Weight Watchers is inextricably linked to Friendly's, and an ice cream cone dripping onto my bare legs in the back seat beside Alison, whose tongue would be stained pink and blue from bleeding gumballs. I don't remember ever associating Bubby's weight with the suffering it must have caused her, the desire that endured, well into her seventies, to lose it.

In the fifteen years I knew her, Bubby only wore dresses. On casual occasions or in her own home, she wore what she called housedresses; for fancier events she was dressed to the nines, in perfectly turned out suits accessorized with pearl or bejeweled pins and clip-on earrings, a matching coat over her shoulder, and highly polished shoes on her dainty feet. Partly this was a reflection of her era. In the 1920s and 1930s, when she was young, only "fast" women wore pants if they wore them at all, and Bubby was always concerned with propriety.

But I suspect in her case the issue was more than decorum. For most of us, clothes become a kind of uniform, designed to showcase or to hide what we like about ourselves or wish to conceal, and the outfits we select contribute to the package being assessed by the outside world in ways both helpful and detrimental. When Bubby died, I was given a jewelry chest in which she kept personal items, one of which was a little gold Weight Watchers pin. I had never seen her wearing it, couldn't imagine anyone wearing a pin proclaiming weight loss, really, but Bubby had kept the pin all those years, and so I kept it too.

WHEN ALISON AND I WERE EIGHT AND NINE, MY MOTHER bought most of our clothes, with our input, if we wanted to give it, which often we did not. If all the kids in my class were wearing, say, Fair Isle sweaters, then I wanted Fair Isle sweaters, but I was generally happy with the clothes my mother brought home. Of course I would often prefer Alison's on principle alone, but when push came to shove, I didn't really care if my sweater was blue and hers green. Colors mattered only in terms of over-arching themes and not to any extreme. Alison had an all-purple birthday party one year, to which we wore matching velvet dresses made by my mother in a wine-like red that she must have hoped Alison would accept as belonging to the purple family. As an unwavering fan of matching (and because it was the early 1980s), I liked color blocks: green pants, navy sweater, green turtleneck, navy headband, green-and-navy canvas bag.

Certain big-ticket items pulled us in—for example, my mother always took us for a back-to-school shopping excursion at the end of the summer, and we both loved picking out a special first-day-of-school dress. In retrospect I may have been a little too out of it in terms of the fashions of the day; I remember quite clearly that on the first day of third grade, I was the only girl in my class wearing a dress—a dress-up dress with a black velvet collar and buttons at that. It is entirely to my mother's credit that I remember this incident not with shame and horror but with fondness, as I was proud of my self-selected dress and comfortable wearing it instead of my usual Levi's cords, which my classmates had stuck to, in spite of my feeling conspicuous. There was also the time I showed up for "jeans night" at my ballroom dancing class wearing a Black Watch plaid dress I'd borrowed from Alison, which stood out like neon against a virtual sea of denim.

Along the lines of her food philosophy, my mother adopted a hands-off policy when it came to clothes; she excluded only ripped or dirty items—they were forbidden with vehemence. Eventually we were too old to fall for the "lost in the laundry" line and I had discovered what I called vintage and my parents called "fit for the trash heap." Before we took over our own wardrobes, however, my mother made it clear that, first and foremost, clothes were what covered your body, that they should be neat and clean and attractive, but that in no way, shape, or form did the price or style of your clothes have anything to do with who or what you were. This was a small clause in one of her basic tenets for living: what a person looked like was wholly uninteresting to my mother. If we were going to waste time worrying about what we looked like—well, she couldn't stop us, but she hoped we knew that she thought it was irrelevant and that she had no intention of participating in the scrutiny. The main problem with this attitude, which I believe was instrumental in forming both Alison's and my sense of self, is that it is contrary to human nature.

To be fair, my mother is the only person I know who does not register a person's physical appearance. I don't know how or why she is like this, and my observation will surely elicit a high degree of skepticism. And yet it's true. It is almost as though she is blind; when she describes a person she has just met, she will never mention a physical quality, even such an obvious trait as quadriplegia or baldness. When I would ask about a student at her school by saying, "Hey, how's the one with the red curly hair?" she would squint and think hard for a moment before answering something like, "Oh, you mean Molly? The artist?" I don't think I have ever heard her call a person *pretty, handsome, fit,* or *attractive,* and it goes without saying that she does not describe appearance with negative adjectives. In fact, she is clearly pained when others do so in front of her, and in my family we don't dish on looks when she's around, although my father, Alison, and I indulge on our own sometimes, well able to live with the guilt. Even at her heaviest, Alison was always willing to take somebody else to task for a terrible haircut or unflattering, too-tight jeans. Once when I expressed surprise at a comment that struck me as particularly harsh, she snapped, "I'm fat, not blind," which shut me up. Now, when she makes occasional disparaging observations about someone's poor judgment in midriff baring or pant size, I bite my tongue, telling myself that it is not the province of the thin to criticize, that being formerly fat does not give Alison a license to sainthood.

The only time I ever heard my mother make an unsolicited comment about somebody's looks—and this is indicative of her disregard for popular culture and its vanities in all forms—was years ago, when we were preparing to watch a rental video of *A Few Good Men*. When the first scene with Tom Cruise played, my mother sat up straighter in her seat and uttered words that have become infamous in our household: "Who's *that* actor? What a nice-looking man!"

OF ALL THE DISAPPROVING LOOKS, MOURNFUL SIGHS, and passive-aggressive comments I directed toward Alison as she began to gain weight, nothing seems as petty or makes me feel quite as ashamed today as the way I behaved over our clothing. Naturally, as Alison grew larger, she grew out of her clothes quickly, and the more weight she gained, the more new clothes she required. I can't fairly imply that I was Cinderella to Alison's spoiled stepsister. I had more clothes, in all the current styles, than most of my peers, thanks to the fact that both my parents enjoyed keeping us well outfitted and that my father is what is known as a clotheshorse. But my clothes were generally purchased in advance, for a reason, such as back to school, formal party, summer job, Christmas, or my birthday, and not just because my mother felt like buying me something new to celebrate a sunny Wednesday.

Every time Alison came home from a shopping trip with my mother and unloaded new pairs of pants, shirts, and sweaters, I felt sick with jealousy, in spite of the knowledge that nobody was happy about these additions to her wardrobe, least of all Alison herself. Did I ever stop to think that Alison would have traded every one of those new elastic-waist pants for my form-fitting Guess jeans with the zippers at the ankles, the kind that came in waist sizes 24 and 25? Probably, but the jealousy would quickly push aside such thoughts. I still remember certain items of clothing Alison was bought for no reason except that she needed something to wear: a pair of pink-and-black plaid pants, a wool blazer in shades of camel and rust that hung in her closet until just a few years ago, never worn.

Worst of all, somehow, were the coats, maybe because some 1950s novel I had read featured a scene in which the co-ed protagonist set off with her mother to a big department store to find the perfect coat to take back east to school. This scene left an indelible impression, and a wool coat became synonymous, for me, with the words *collegiate, sophistication,* and *style.* When I went with my

mother to buy my first grown-up coat—a long wool version that I would choose myself and that didn't have a
velvet collar and hooks for mittens inside the sleeves—I
agonized over the selection and finally narrowed it down
to two: a camel's-hair with a belt at the waist and a single-
breasted nubby brown tweed.

I went with the tweed, largely, I suspect, because the
girl in my 1950s book had chosen tweed and because
it seemed both worldly and bohemian. I could picture
Sylvia Plath in a tweed coat, for example, maybe with
neat little gloves that would poke endearingly out of her
pockets when the weather got warm. For the first year,
I wore my brown tweed coat almost every day, if there
was even so much as a breeze. I am afraid it preceded
Columbus Day and wore out its welcome by Memorial
Day, and when the following winter rolled around, the
last thing I wanted to do was put it on again. I wanted a
new winter coat.

I didn't push too hard. My role was to sit quietly in the
boat and try to counteract any rocking with implacable
calm. There was also the fact that my tweed coat was still
in excellent shape, in spite of hard use, and that it had
been purchased with the understanding that it would last
me for the next couple of years. Unlike Alison, I also
had a parka for skiing and a windbreaker shell from my
soccer team, as well as a denim jacket and a suede car
coat from a thrift store; all these items were hard to find
in extralarge sizes. Over the previous couple of years,
Alison had acquired coats at the rate of two a winter. For

a New England winter, coats need to fit—they need to close all the way and they need sleeves loose enough for mobility and sufficiently long to cover the wrists. They also must be, at least in one incarnation, nice enough to wear over a dress to a special occasion, when a puffy down jacket with dirt splotches from making snow angels in the driveway just won't do. My mother felt strongly about this, which was part of the reason I'd been taken to buy a real coat myself. She felt so strongly about this that when Alison outgrew a coat or refused to wear one because she didn't like the way it fit, she would eventually end up with another. I coveted each addition, tried it on when she wasn't home, although, in one way or another, it would be too big: a dark green, trapeze-shaped, knee-length one from a popular catalog, a formal black one with a small notched collar, and a charcoal gray one with deep pockets and a soft, lush nap.

One Christmas Eve, as we set out for a holiday party, Alison walked out the door and toward the car coatless, dressed in one of the black skirts and sweaters that had become her uniform. The outfit was borderline appropriate for a holiday gathering, but since we were still in high school, my choice of attire was also only marginally suitable for dress-up. My mother looked displeased but didn't ask us to go back and change. I was wearing my tweed coat, not to make my mother happy but because it was freezing outside, and I would not have thought to leave the house without it. Alison didn't care about the weather. There were many days she set out for school wearing no socks, even when a foot of snow covered the ground. My mother had few rules in general, but the ones she made she preferred we adhere to without argument or modification. One was that if we were going some place public with her, we needed to be dressed acceptably, which meant wearing a coat, and a decent one at that.

"Alison, do you want me to get you your gray coat?" my mother asked, trying to keep her voice even. My father was already in the car, warming it up, probably placing bets with himself as to how late we would be and preparing his shopworn speech for our host about how he'd been ready early and our tardiness wasn't his fault. I sat primly on the couch in the family room facing the front door, my hands in the deep pockets of my now-hated tweed. As my collie knows hours in advance of a rainstorm, I could sense when Alison was building up to a temper tantrum; I knew it was too soon to join my dad in the car.

"I'm not wearing that coat," Alison said tonelessly, indicating, to me, the tumult to come. They went back and forth in this vein for a few minutes, until my father flung open the door, his exasperation filling the room.

"We're already ten minutes late," he seethed, noting first me, silent and still on the couch, and then Alison and my mother, in their standoff. Once my father got involved, I knew the evening was shot. He and Alison were already well on their way to perfecting what would become their master dance of poking at each other's weak spots, a dance—like all great ones—encompassing two partners tailor-made for each other.

Eventually Alison screamed, "Fine! I will go get that stupid coat and wear it if that's what you want!" I could tell from the scream's progressive fade that she was going down to the basement, although this seemed odd, as the coat closet was in the entryway. When she came back upstairs, after a suspiciously long time had passed, she held out the coat to my mother. My father had gone back to the car, afraid, as always, that a marauding bandit would appear in our rural neck of the woods and steal it out from under him if it was left unlocked and unattended for more than fifteen seconds in the driveway.

I heard my mother's sharp intake of breath, Alison's silence in response. I opened my book and started to read, a neat trick I had developed as a defense mechanism. (To this day I can read anywhere at all with perfect comprehension: standing on a crowded city bus, walking down the street, probably in the throes of the apocalypse.) With that characteristic mix of boldness, recklessness, and ingenuity that always flooded me with shock and envy, Alison had taken shears to her coat. The garment was still in one piece, but she'd made cuts in enough places that it was totally unwearable, as well as unrestorable. Alison would not be wearing her gray coat that evening, although I knew my mother well enough to suspect that Alison was already regretting this dramatic action. My mother, and then Alison—the bluster gone—in one of her other, perfectly acceptable coats, filed out the front door. I shut my book carefully, folding over one corner of a page to mark my place, and followed them, locking the door, as my father watched from the front seat of the idling car to make sure I did so.

I don't think Alison ever fully understood how upset I was every time she got new clothes, and I think to the extent that she did, she thought my distress was about the clothes themselves. The truth is that I craved the extra attention, especially from my mother, who doled it out less indiscriminately than my father and was highly sensitive to pettiness on my part. My father also gave Alison extra attention, a heartfelt mixture of protective instincts, conspiratorial advice, and watchful, nagging monitoring. As he had experience with weight gain himself and through his mother, he understood Alison's struggles, failures, and triumphs better than we did. He knew firsthand what the world saw when it looked at a fat person, and would have done anything to prevent Alison from being viewed with disapproving eyes. In spite of the fact that she was constantly yelling at him to stop telling her what to eat and what not to, or accusing him of staring at her while she was eating, in a way she tolerated such behavior from him more readily than she did from me; his pestering stemmed from real-life experience, while my mother could offer only solace and advice, and I could not see a tree of empathy for the forest of sibling rivalry I was generally lost in. In fact, although Alison talked about her weight with my mother, sometimes, and with me, rarely, my father was her primary sounding board, as well as shooting range and firing squad. Sometimes I would be sitting alone in the back seat of the car on an even-numbered day, feeling like a foreign exchange student while they laughingly debated roast chicken versus turkey as a high-protein, low-fat entrée or shouted at each other about whether Alison should have eaten two hot dogs at the previous night's Celtics game.

IN SPITE OF THE FACT THAT ALISON AND I DID NOT generally talk about weight, mine or hers, and that I was unreasonably jealous of her clothing and the attention it drew from my parents, Alison and I often went clothes shopping together, and some of the time it was actually fun. (Alison claims, now, that she hates shopping with me because I am loath to make a decision, but I think she doth protest too much, as she is often the first to suggest an excursion and these days enjoys trying on virtually everything in a given store, regardless of her intentions to purchase.) When we were teenagers and in our early twenties, however, we were primarily shopping for me. I am not blind to the fact that these outings were fraught for Alison, in ways they were not for me. But it is true that Alison liked picking out clothes for me, whether or not I was around—her birthday and Christmas gifts to me were almost always, and still are, something to wear. When we were together, I suspect, she was actually shopping, in her head, for Alison—that thin, theoretical Alison who would burst on the scene at some unspecified date in the future—and that I was a sorry but useful approximation. In a dressing room, Alison never hesitated to tell me, even as she was assessing on me the outfits of her choosing, that if only she were thin, they would look infinitely better on her. She was ruthless about my appearance, criticizing the way certain colors brought out my freckles or my pale skin, certain styles accentuated my too long torso or made me look short. And my taste! In Alison's opinion, the clothes I bought for myself were bland, unflattering, too trendy, not trendy enough—the wrong color, cut, cloth, or all three.

As when she took a wooden spoon from my hand and salvaged a dish I was cooking, when Alison appeared from behind a rack with a skirt in my size, I generally tried it on, fighting the urge to leave her in a locked dressing room until the cleaning staff showed up to release her. Why would I follow her advice? Because in addition to her artistic talent and sense of aesthetics, all those years envisioning her idealized self in her idealized wardrobe had left Alison with an uncanny ability to determine what would look best on others, especially me. Naturally sloppy, I had never spent much time thinking about what would look good on me, and why or why not. She was more conscious of flattering cuts, knew when a smaller or larger size would change the shape of an outfit. At Christmas I would open a gift from her—such as a zebra-striped skirt in black and royal blue with a fitted black sweater—and think, "Hell will freeze over before I am caught dead in this skirt." I would picture the black sweater with jeans, or my ancient, threadbare Levi's cords—the same style I'd worn every day in the third grade. And then, sure enough, I would be invited to a party, and after throwing every item of clothing I owned on the top of a pile consisting largely of corduroy, I would put on that crazy skirt and get more compliments on it than anything I'd ever worn before.

Alison would tell you herself that she has a great eye. In fact, she would probably be happy to inform you if what you are wearing is flattering or if you should steer away from pencil skirts, no matter what the saleswoman tells you at Saks. In this, she is reminiscent of my great-aunt, the one with the eternal bouffant and the running monologue on your personal hair history. Alison knows that she sees the world differently from most people, partly because she is an artist, and artists see planes and colors and gradations the rest of us don't; they are visual before their other senses kick in. And Alison has always been someone who *sees*; this is a gift she inherited from a long line of women.

My mother, a passionate shell collector, can spend hours and hours walking a beach and picking up specimens. She has such an eye for it after so many years of experience that she discards nine out of ten "gets," deeming only the very best shells worthy of her exclusive net. My grandmother walks, too, but not as far these days. When her legs get tired, she sits on the sand where the tiny shells camouflage themselves and sifts through handfuls, patient in a way that only time can make you, selecting the perfect miniatures for her little glass boxes and treasure chests. But Alison. Alison can walk longer than my mother, sift more patiently than Mormor. Even as a small child, when I would lose interest after ten minutes flat, she would always emerge with the one shell my mother and grandmother had coveted for years, hold her arm up, triumphant, from a mile down one stretch of beach.

Alison can look at a pile of stones on a beach and pluck out an iridescent moonshadow shell from the shape it makes under its blanket of sand. She can spot the point of a whelk poking out from a distance at which most people can't even identify shapes. A few years ago, when those "magic sight" books were popular, the ones in which you stared at an image made up of hundreds of colored shapes out of which—if you were looking in just the right way—a marvelous scene of a dragon would appear, my mother acquired a bunch of them. One Christmas we sat, my extended family, passing them around and squinting in frustration. No matter how hard I squinted, all I saw were little blobs. I was starting to give myself a headache. When Alison appeared in the room after we'd been staring and squinting for half an hour or so, my mother held up one of the books.

"What's this, Ali?" she asked, and Alison adjusted her glasses and came over to where my mother was sitting.

"It's a carnival," she said, matter-of-factly, "with rides and balloons," and walked out again without a backward glance.

It is a gift to be able to see. It is also a gift to be able to see the possibility and potential in others, and Alison has been blessed with both gifts. Even when she is angry with or feels hurt by me, the person she sees when she looks at me is someone I usually am not but would very much like to be. It is not only *my* best self Alison is capable of eliciting, although she prefers reflecting on my worst. Like many people who have suffered in some capacity, she has a sharp eye for anyone being underestimated or somehow on the outside of things. Like our mother, she is willing to give just about anybody a chance, and more often than not people live up to her expectations.

Unfortunately, during the years in which she grew to weigh over three hundred pounds, Alison lost sight of herself.

FOUR

weight and lightness

When we were children, Alison loved to be photographed. I liked it, too, but was shyer about it, more
self-conscious by far. In many of our family photos, especially the posed ones of us both, I recognize what everyone
in my family calls my fake smile. It extends high at the
corners of my mouth, which appear to be aspiring to
reach the tops of my ears in a manner similar to that of
the Joker whenever Batman appears. I have always been
self-conscious about my teeth, so I avoid allowing them
to make even the briefest appearance on film, and my
eyes are disengaged from the process altogether, enhanc-
ing the feeling of disconnect, as—at least to me—they
often look worried, in contrast to the unnatural glee of
the mouth. Beside me, Alison always looks happy with a

joy that reaches her eyes. Her mouth is usually open, either because she was talking while the picture was taken or because her head is thrown back in laughter. Maybe this is just my perspective, coloring the lens through which I am viewing the photographs. But when I look through our early family albums, I see movement and life in Alison's image, an irrepressible vitality in her limbs and expression.

We have a video of us at five and six, which brings this contrast into three dimensions, provides a glimpse into a dynamic whose roots have been buried by time. In it we sit side by side on a piano bench while I hunch over the keys, concentration evident in my back and shoulders. You can't see my hands on the piano itself, but when I watch the video, I can see them, in my mind's eye, arched high, "high enough to put an orange under," the way our piano teacher had instructed. Making for a most dissonant duet, Alison pounds away heartily next to me, her head swaying to a rhythm only she can hear. Later, as we are opening Christmas presents, I sit prettily, smoothing my long flannel nightgown around my legs. I roll my eyes at my former self. I know I was imagining how I looked, how the scene around me looked, so rapt in my thoughts that I was barely paying attention to either the camera or the gift I was opening. On the other side of the tree, meanwhile, Alison is ripping paper with gusto, laughing with her entire squirming body.

"Mom! Dad!" she shouts repeatedly. "Are you sure this will be on the video?" She flirts blatantly with the camera, holding each gift up to it with coy lowered eyelids. "I *love* this," she gushes, before tossing whatever it is over her shoulder. And then, "Are you looking at me, guys? Are you watching me?" Finally, at the end of the video, when you can tell we are all losing steam, camera operator and subjects alike, Alison speaks again, so faintly that I've never been sure if she actually said the words or I am making them up, although by now I have watched the clip many times. The tone is different, not coy or flirtatious but earnest. "Amo?" I always forget how early she started calling me that. "Do you want to come see what I got?"

Once Alison started to gain weight, and through all the years she was fat, her relationship to cameras of all kinds—to documentation itself—became antagonistic. In photos from those years, she is either standing behind the rest of us, her head partially visible over two people's shoulders, or seated with a pillow on her lap, in an attempt to conceal her stomach. Once in a great while she would want to be photographed; she'd make the rest of us wait as she arranged herself in exactly the position she had in mind and would snap at you if you so much as jostled her after she'd established it. Most of the time, however, she simply refused, and my father, who couldn't quite give up on his annual favorites, would wheedle. If he managed to capture an image not to Alison's liking, it would often disappear from the album if it ever got that far in the first place.

Alison used to look at these rare pictures of herself with a peculiar expression, and I could never tell if she was surveying herself with disgust or questioning their validity. Maybe it was a little of both. As we got older, though, and Alison grew to hate being captured on film, I became increasingly open to it, partly, I suspect, to deflect the tension that rose in us all at the sight of a camera. If I stood smiling where I was supposed to, and smiled hard enough, then maybe I would cancel out the black hole where Alison either glared at the camera or refused to so much as appear.

IT WAS DURING HIGH SCHOOL THAT ALISON BECAME obese, began overeating in earnest, sometimes in front of the rest of us, rarely at school, and usually in the privacy of her bedroom. Most of the memories I conjure up of her at that time take place in that room, a pink-and-yellow bower that suited her childhood persona, not the new and unfamiliar one who primarily wore black and attached a lock to her door one day when I was out—two locks, actually, a padlock on the outside and a latch with a hook to keep us out when she was inside. The only rooms in our house with locks were the bathrooms. We had never had an occasion to want them; my parents believed in respecting our privacy, and Alison and I left each other alone when we thought it was important to do so. The locks were the beginning of a period in Alison's life that somewhat resembled imprisonment.

Melodramatic? Sure. But so was lying under my bed seeing how still I could keep my body as my parents talked at Alison through that locked door. They had decided she should see a psychiatrist, not directly because of her weight problem but because it was making her so unhappy. I could have warned my parents what her reaction to this suggestion would be, although I was uncomfortable using that kind of language in front of them. We weren't a big "psychiatrist" family. At that time, I didn't know anyone who had been to one, and although I didn't say this to my parents or to Alison, I thought their decision was pretty extreme. In my opinion, Alison didn't have any psychiatric issues; all she needed to do was lose weight, and then she would like high school more, join a sports team, have friends over to study for tests and work on school projects, wake up before noon on weekends, and stop hiding food in her closet and under her bed. I never got to spend time in her closet anymore, although it was as special a place as it ever had been. By this point she was using it more as the walk-in clothes receptacle it was intended to be, but because its owner was Alison, it still resembled a miniature room. She had arranged an intricate wire tree with twirling branches on one wall for hanging jewelry, which—like makeup and shoes—she collected in extravagant amounts in the years she was fat. During high school Alison also acquired what had to be the world's largest collection of nail polish.

The locks threw my parents for a loop, served as a wake-up call of sorts. They had never exactly forbidden locks on the doors, but it was extremely inconvenient to be denied access to Alison, except at her whim. I found the situation difficult, too, but although my feelings were hurt, I didn't consider counteracting with a lock for my room. I wanted *her* to come *out*, not to stay in my room. Before too long, I figured out that my age-old tactic of playing hard to get was no longer working. Alison didn't miss me when I wasn't knocking at her door. If the lock didn't get the message across, her crossed arms and tight voice did, whenever she emerged. She wanted to be left alone. I understood this, to a certain extent. I spent most of my seventeenth year lying on my bedroom floor staring up at the ceiling, with the cat on my chest, listening to the Rolling Stones' *Flowers* album over and over, especially "Ruby Tuesday." I would sing along in my off-key tenor, wondering why nobody understood that I, too, needed to be free—which was why they should let me borrow the car whenever I wanted, surely what Mick Jagger had meant in an indirect kind of a way. But even I could recognize that Alison's desire for solitude had a quality that went beyond teenage angst and egocentrism. She seemed almost lost inside herself, and when I would look at her too hard, she would look away, not wanting to be seen.

Eventually, and I don't remember how, my parents got her to go to a psychiatrist. Alison denies this, but I remember vividly how she stuck it to all of them; my parents' frustrated if gradual submission to her, and, as always, my awe at her indomitable will. My father had purchased one of those miniature, battery-operated television sets, probably for some sports-related reason, but Alison, who had fallen in love with television although we weren't allowed to watch much, co-opted the set soon after it appeared, and the TV could usually be found in her room. Each time she was taken to the psychiatrist's office in Boston, a trip she made with our dad, she would bring it along. During the hour-long session, she would watch a soap opera, not because she was a fan but because soap operas were the only programs on in the late afternoon. For an entire year—she told me this at the time, surprised, I think, by her own stamina—she did not utter a single word in the psychiatrist's office. I can picture this, down to the most minute detail: a middle-age man, practiced in the art of closed-off adolescents, watching Alison ignore him in favor of afternoon trysts and identical twins returned from the grave. Finally, the psychiatrist gave in. He told my parents they were wasting their money, a point I had been belaboring all year. Alison was relieved, but she did miss the unusual hot dogs wrapped in Syrian bread, sold at a stand outside the hospital entrance, which she and my dad had stopped for after each appointment.

THE SPRING OF HER FRESHMAN YEAR OF HIGH SCHOOL was the first time Alison signed up for Diet Center, and by the fall she had lost over fifty pounds. Now she will say that the reason she gained the weight back during the

following year was that she had lost it to please her coun-
selor at the center and not for herself, but chances are
good it had more to do with that particular malady we
call being fifteen. According to Alison, she received a lot
more attention when school resumed that fall. Girls
asked her if she would start going to parties, the implica-
tion being now that she was thin. (One has to wonder
about the happiness quotient of those girls who weren't
going to parties and didn't have a weight problem as their
excuse, real or projected.) When I asked Alison recently
why she had not tried Diet Center again during high
school, since it had been successful the first time, her
answer surprised me.

"I was happier being heavy," she said, and involuntarily
I amended this sentiment.

"You mean you *thought* you were happier," I said,
although I found even this answer confusing.

"No, I *was* happier," she said firmly. "If I hadn't been
fat, I would have had to hang out with those girls."

Alison may have thought she was happier being heavy
in high school, and for all I know, she actually was. I
suspect, however, that she was not happier but more
comfortable—with a body that had become a kind of dis-
guise, familiarity breeding not contempt, exactly, but
complacency. Fat, Alison didn't have to deal with the
social anxiety and pressure that makes many people look
back at high school with lingering animosity. Fat, she was
able to exist in a sort of private, alternate universe, going
to classes, immersing herself in her artwork and honing

her skills, hanging out with a few close friends and her family if she felt like it, but mostly spending time alone in her room.

I'm not sure if things would have been different had Alison chosen a different high school; the exclusive single-sex prep school she attended attracted a largely shallow, materialistic, boy- and sports-crazy group of girls. As far as I can tell, only one good thing emerged from this place: Alison realized she was not just talented but actually an artist. One of the art teachers recognized in Alison an originality lacking in most of his students and took an interest in her, encouraging her to sign up for additional art electives and allowing her to use the studios and supplies at all times. Soon she was designing the posters and programs for most of the school's productions. I will admit, for the sake of full disclosure, that I am the kind of person who would attend a high school musical even if I didn't know anyone involved, but I was so excited the year Alison's school put on *Grease* that I invited two of my closest friends at college to come to Massachusetts to attend with me. The show was quite good, actually; apparently some of the whiny girls I'd heard about and met had acting ability and could carry a tune.

As I hummed along with the songs, trying not to sing out loud, a bad habit I've been chided for more than once, my eyes kept wandering off the stage and down to the program, where Alison's name appeared in print. Sometimes I felt as though my friends condescended to Alison, treated her as if she were fragile and delicate instead of fat. This skeptical interpretation may say more about me than about my friends; it was not just Alison who could be paranoid about how others treated her. I may well have seen patronizing smiles where only friendly curiosity existed. There was no doubt, however, that my friends were impressed by Alison's artwork, especially the enormous posters she'd silk-screened of Sandy and Danny dancing in the moonlight, which were posted all over the school. If Alison was drawing inward, her shoulders stooped in her flowing black clothes, her artwork looked increasingly outward: colors and shapes on a grand, exuberant scale.

Such nights were infrequent. Alison had never accompanied me to events at my high school. I don't think she ever sat in the bleachers to watch me play basketball— which, all things considered, may well have been for the best. When my soccer and lacrosse teams visited Alison's school for away games, I had to hunt her down if I wanted to see her, and usually I just didn't bother. Sometimes I would tell the girl I was guarding that my sister went to the school and ask if she knew her, but I was so proactively angry at the expression I imagined she would make that more often I did not. I remember once, just before a lacrosse game, a girl with a long black ponytail came up to me and asked if I was Alison's sister.

"Yes," I answered warily, standing straight and trying to look as confident as was possible in cleats and a miniskirt kilt.

"Wow. You guys don't look anything alike," she said,

and I turned, my face hot, and walked to the shade of a tree by the side of the field, away from my teammates, who hadn't been listening anyway.

WHEN I LEFT FOR COLLEGE, MY RELATIONSHIP WITH Alison improved immediately, as so often happens with siblings, especially those close in age who have been staking claim to the same patch of battlefield for so long. Our newfound camaraderie was a function of several factors, including the freedom the distance gave us to exist outside the context of our relationship. I had been assigned to a one-room triple, which meant, essentially, that I shared an odd-shaped room with two other girls. During the first week, amid my panic and excitement, I couldn't fight the uneasy feeling each night that something was off. It finally occurred to me as I lay in bed wide awake, staring at the ceiling and listening to my roommates breathing in tandem, wondering if I knew them well enough yet to wake them up. Never before had I spent more than a week or two away from Alison, and I could count those occasions on the fingers of one hand. For the next four years (I couldn't imagine beyond them), I was truly on my own.

Artists know that negative space can be even more powerful than an image itself. When you are learning to draw, in fact, a good instructor will often ask you to sketch something by drawing around it, creating its borders by shading in not the object but the air pushing into it.

Throughout college, but especially that first semester, I was aware of Alison's absence—not constantly, like pain, but every so often in the back of my mind, like the memory of pain. Don't get me wrong; I wasn't indulging in soft-color daydreams about special experiences Alison and I had shared. I didn't miss arguing with her about who had stolen whose turquoise necklace, or being locked out of her bedroom when I knew she had something of mine in there, or hearing the click that indicated her presence at the other end of one of my phone conversations. I didn't miss sitting monklike in a room while she sucked out all the energy, commanded the attention of everyone in her vicinity while I cringed. And I didn't miss the darkness that had enveloped her over the previous couple of years, the inward turn that had also carried her further from me, which I suspected she would have to correct on her own. But did I miss her, so much that I was truly surprised.

During our first awkward phone call, it became clear that she missed me, too, maybe not in quite the same way but with a similar intensity and surprise; knowing how she felt made me feel less alone. And on my first trip home that fall, I could sense a change in Alison, a change for the better. She was still in her black garb and heavy black boots, but there was a lightness to the way she held up her head and in her eyes, and I knew, on some level, that had something to do with me, with my absence. On her own, Alison did not have to claw for our parents' attention; in fact, she began *not* to want it, to try to escape from their scrutiny, the way most teenagers do early on. Without me to live up to or resent, she had started to think about what else she could live up to, what she wanted to do. She told me, that Christmas break, that she had decided to apply to the Rhode Island School of Design, the most prestigious art school in the country, and I held myself back from pointing out that our parents would insist on the liberal arts, that she could pursue art after college or as part of her course of studies. In the past, she would have sensed my tacit disapproval and lashed out, but she just smiled at my tight expression, tossed her hair over her shoulder.

"Mom and Dad think it's a great idea," she said. "And I can take classes at Brown, too."

The following fall, when I was home for October break, my parents and I drove to Providence so I could see Alison and RISD. I had never been to Providence before, although it was close to our house, and I couldn't help feeling a little jealous as we drove up and down the streets looking for parking. Poughkeepsie, where I went to school, is not a college town. The campus, in spite of students' annual, valiant attempts to build bridges with the community, is a self-sustaining microcosm, and the few businesses we frequented off campus were chain stores and fast food restaurants that could have been anywhere. Providence looked like Harvard Square but better. Every street had clothing boutiques and cafés, bars, and restaurants, and as we crossed the street to Alison's dorm, I thought about the abandoned storefronts and decrepit

pharmacies on the only commercial street in walking distance of the school I had chosen. As we entered, students
looked at us curiously, the way students do when anybody's family arrives, and I found myself staring right
back. I had gone to an extremely artsy high school; when
I'd first visited, in fact, my tour guide sported a royal blue
Mohawk, which I took as a positive sign, although certainly terrifying. And Vassar, in the 1990s, was hardly the
bastion of afternoon teas and ladies in gloves that most of
my relatives seemed to envision. Of all the colleges I had
looked at, its students had been the most unconvention-
ally appealing to me. But RISD was the major leagues.
Some of the kids drinking coffee in the student lounge
appeared to be wearing costumes—top hats or petticoats;
others had dreadlocks, shaved heads, or hoops in their
noses. I had fancied my cutoff leggings under a lopped-off
skirt and my thrift-store sweater with a stranger's mono-
gram to be quite avant-garde; I'd dressed for Alison, as
was often the case. But suddenly I felt mousy and suburban; the sensation would endure around Alison's friends
for years to come.

As the elevator doors opened, I could hear Alison
screaming with laughter from behind a closed door all
the way at the end of the hallway. When she flung open
the door in response to my tentative knock, I almost
didn't recognize her. Her body looked exactly the same. If
anything, she had possibly gained a little weight. But her
demeanor was so changed—her hair brighter and wavy
and wild, her clothes multitextured and not entirely

black, her smile enormous and with so much of its old insouciance—that I looked back at my parents, a little nervous. How had this happened so fast? That day Alison walked us around the dorm to meet her new friends, who were so plentiful I couldn't keep track of names and faces and kept thinking she was introducing me to the same person for the third or fourth time. Everybody knew her, greeted her with that pleasure she'd elicited so effortlessly back in elementary school, when kids on the playground at recess would ask me if she was my sister, because they hoped I could give them some kind of "in." Then she took us to the studios, open cubicles in the ceramics department, which she explained were RISD students' second dorm rooms.

The following year, when Alison was assigned her own studio, even this boxlike workspace soon looked like somewhere I'd want to hang out. I could only imagine where she'd found the armchair, with its chicly faded upholstery, the little colored lights strung along the wall, the lamps and art books and old-fashioned radio, covered with a fine gray dust I recognized as clay from Alison's childhood art classes at the De Cordova Museum and the pottery shed at my high school.

At the time of the first visit, however, all I could think was that Alison had gone from a bad school, for her anyway, to one that could have been designed on her behalf. Now I realize she had found a community in which she could emerge from the folds of her clothing, return, at least partway, to the self she had buried under all that extra weight. This transformation made a lot of sense. First, there was the change of environment, from her childhood home, where her role had become so deeply ingrained, to an uncharted territory, where she could carve out a new role, or reclaim one she could have had but for the rest of us, by which I mean mostly me. At college many eighteen-year-olds, away from their families for the first time, discover new selves. In Alison's case, her reemergence also had something to do with her distance from me, as I've mentioned. At RISD, Alison wasn't my sister; she was only herself.

Alison thrived at RISD for the whole four years, if thriving means throwing expansive, overattended parties that attracted upperclassmen and even professors; accumulating a group of dazzlingly talented friends whose hobbies were blowing glass and forging iron; having disruptive romantic entanglements with glamorous men from foreign countries for whom, as far as I could tell, her weight was not an issue; and—for an assignment—designing a set of dishes for one of Providence's best restaurants. Near the end of her senior year, my parents and I went back to RISD, along with Mormor, my aunt and uncle, and a couple of cousins, for Alison's Senior Show. When I walked into the gallery space, pulling at my uncharacteristically straight skirt and tottering slightly in new high-heeled shoes, I spotted Alison across the room, her back to me, as she spoke to an unfamiliar man. I saw that one of the bowls from her latest series was on a pedestal next to her, and I wondered if the man was a professor, an artist himself, and felt nervous on her behalf—did she mind watching as an expert appraised her work?

I wandered over to the area where the rest of her work was displayed. That year she had been making platters and bowls, but mostly bowls—lacy, Asian-influenced creations that were somehow airy and sturdy at the same time, fired in a soothing sage green, a pale milky yellow. Some of the platters had gold rubbed into them, which gave them an elegant sheen, like a treasure in the dim light of a Turkish palace. I couldn't help but think of Alison's unorthodox approach to our childhood coloring books and the coiled pots I had made in elementary school—smooth, uniform, and lifeless. Before acknowledging how stunning these shimmering bowls were, how distinctive, how precious, I had this thought: there's no way I could ever have made them.

As the man walked away from Alison to where another student stood with his family amid his creations, I finally approached her. She looked pleased to see me, not nervous at all.

"Was that a professor?" I asked, trying not to stare at the man.

"I don't know," she shrugged. "He was just asking me about a certain technique." I waited for her to ask me what I thought about her work; Alison always sought my opinion, even when I knew she didn't want to. "Where are Mom and Dad?" she inquired instead, turning away from me.

AFTER COLLEGE, ALISON WENT HOME TO MY PARENTS'
house in Massachusetts. My graduation gift from our parents had been a laptop computer; Alison's was a wheel
and a kiln, which still sit in their basement today. But Alison seemed to lose interest in ceramics not long after
graduation—she was more interested than I'd ever been
in having new experiences, trying new things. Unlike me,
she didn't seem concerned with launching a career,
expressed no anxiety about her status in the world at
large. She worked at a design store for a while but grew
frustrated selling dishes and housewares. She was a waitress at a place in Boston's South End but found the job
excruciatingly boring until she convinced the owner to
let her take over some of the food preparation. This capti-
vated her for a while, especially as most of the customers
began requesting her dishes exclusively. A friend of mine
who was living in the area told me one day that she'd
discovered the best cake she'd ever had, and I knew, without having to ask, that it was Alison's. Then, in a leap I
never would have made but envied tremendously, Alison
announced she was moving to London with a friend who
had musical ambitions and that she was going to find
work in a restaurant kitchen.

In London, Alison found not only an apartment she
could afford on next to nothing but a job at a big, popular
restaurant, doing prep work for the chefs. The work was

grueling, but she loved the other kitchen employees and the frenzied pace; at night she and her friend would frequent gay discos, where she would sometimes moonlight as a coat-check girl and where she once met Boy George. She claimed that the British were less weight-conscious than Americans, that she had never felt better about her body, although she was not losing weight. I was working in publishing, wearing blazers to my office and carrying a leather briefcase; in weak protest, however, I refused to wear sneakers to walk to the subway, and then change to office-style shoes when I got to work as many women did; I could only imagine Alison's scorn. At Christmas the first year she was away, I spent weeks looking for the perfect gift to send her from New York. She wouldn't be coming home to Sudbury; the trip would be too expensive and besides, she had to work—"Restaurants don't take vacations," she chided, when I begged her to come home. I had never spent a major holiday apart from her.

After buying a few things and returning them, I walked into a store on Broadway one day on a whim and saw a hat box that zipped around the top. The leather was soft and richly colored brown, and it smelled like leather is supposed to but rarely does. It was an odd gift, to be sure, and I was uncertain what a person would do with a leather hat box, but if anyone would have an idea, Alison would. I bought it, although it cost much more than I'd planned on spending, and I had to send it to London in a huge package, which ate up the rest of my holiday budget, but all day that Christmas I kept waiting for the phone to ring. When she finally called, I stood by impatiently as my parents each talked to her. I wasn't going to ask about it, I had decided.

"That was the best present *ever*," she shouted into the phone as soon as she heard my voice, and I realized with a pang how much I had cared that she like it, how much I wanted her home. Over the years, Alison has frequently extorted, bribed, tortured, and otherwise threatened my sanity with her schemes or adventures, but she has also fixed me in ways that only she could. I will never forget the cold December afternoon in the mid-1990s when I telephoned her—and only her—from the futon I used as a couch in my grad school apartment to tell her that Ben, my boyfriend, then, of six years and now my husband, had called to say he was breaking up with me, that he thought we wanted, in modern-day parlance, "different things." It was one of those one-sided, blubbering, incomprehensible conversations. She told me I would be fine, which was all I needed to hear right then. When I felt that I could breathe normally again, I thanked her for listening and hung up, but immediately remembered something I had forgotten to tell her. I called back, and for a few seconds thought I had reached a wrong number: she was crying so hard she couldn't speak, weeping, really, and the intensity of her sadness for me, combined with the protective instincts that had enabled her to wait until I'd hung up the phone, surprised me, although it shouldn't have. Alison has always been able to offer comfort in a selfless way.

When Alison came back from London—only because of work-visa issues—she played around for a while at a few jobs, but it seemed clear after her restaurant experience that she should be cooking. The Culinary Institute of America is near Vassar, and as a student I'd had a few outstanding meals there. I called and had the institute send Alison an application, but she told me she wanted a job. After a while she found one at a prestigious catering company in Boston's South End and, before long, became one of its chefs. Today she cooks meals for two hundred people in an industrial kitchen or works with servers and other chefs at parties in private homes and formal events for individuals and corporations, everything from Nantucket weddings to a celebration of Armani's new perfume.

I REMEMBER FEELING TREMENDOUS RELIEF AS EARLY as my first trip to RISD, when I sensed the darkness of Alison's teenage years lifting and dissipating. I confess that this relief was partly selfish, as I was more than ready to have a sister who wouldn't refuse, even if she was in a bad mood, to acknowledge my friends when they said hello to her, who would meet me for drinks on a Saturday night in a public venue and introduce me to the people she cared about, most of whom I didn't really know. While she had had boyfriends before, the relationships often ended dramatically, leaving her frustrated and angry. I felt confident her reborn personality would increase her chances for a positive one. I was also relieved for my parents, who had seemed darker, too, when Alison did, weighed down by the frustration of not being able to help. Each time my mother told me that Alison would have to want to lose weight badly enough in order to do so, that no one other than Alison could make Alison lose weight, I understood the toll this admission took on my mother. I am not yet a parent, but already I know there is nothing worse than seeing your child suffer. And I was relieved for Alison, who finally seemed willing to see that being fat did not have to mean having no life.

It was only when she talked about her future as a thin person that I worried about Alison now. There was never an ounce of uncertainty in her assertions. She was not hopeful, wishful, or even wistful. Rather, she would examine a new skirt of mine, appraise it with those all-seeing eyes. "This will look great on me when I'm thin," she would say. "Hold onto this one." I knew better than to enter into a discussion, to suggest what I was thinking: that she wasn't magically going to lose almost two hundred pounds, that it was highly unlikely she would wake up one morning and suddenly be able to fit into my skirt. Every so often, when she was in a really good mood, I would mention a great gym one of my friends in Boston had joined or say, ever so casually, that I was trying to incorporate more fruits and vegetables into my diet. After fifteen years of being fat, though, Alison felt she had earned the right to ignore such veiled suggestions, especially from me. In fact, she would usually follow up her initial vision of herself with a second one, even more unreasonably optimistic, in my mind—considering that she was no longer on any kind of a diet and was unwilling even to consider an exercise program.

"Yes, I'll wear miniskirts when I'm thin. With knee-high boots," she would say, and I would keep my expression neutral, clumsily changing the subject.

Alison never asked me directly if I thought she would ever lose weight. Maybe she asked our parents, or her friends, but she never asked me. If she had, I would have lied to her without flinching, but my heart would have ached in my chest. I didn't think she'd ever be thin.

As much as I wanted Alison to lose weight, as much as I willed her to abstain when I caught her overeating or discovered evidence that she had been, I never thought of her as one of a pack, as part of a widespread problem. I didn't associate her with television news programs featuring obese suicidal shut-ins, or magazine articles pushing slim-down shakes and metabolism tablets, or even people I encountered in real life: men and women on the bus, or in the grocery store, whose weight attracted negative attention from onlookers and clearly interfered with their comfort or happiness.

A fat person is not a statistic, a dot on a graph. A fat person is somebody who once twirled in front of a camera like a movie star on the red carpet and now cuts herself out of a photograph because she can't bear to see what she looks like. A fat person is someone who once drew a crowd when she opened her lunch box or stepped off the school bus and now barely comes out of her bedroom. A fat person is somebody's little sister.

FIVE

transformation

I had surgery once, at twenty-one, when my impacted wisdom teeth were removed. The experience was disorienting, from the long wait on an orange plastic chair at the hospital, to the blur of the anesthesia, to the wheelchair in which I was pushed to my mother's waiting car, the only wheelchair I have sat in. The days immediately after the surgery are lost; I was put on Percocet for the pain, which was substantial, fell asleep as soon as I collapsed on my bed and woke up—or realized I was awake, as I'd been taking the pills all along—later in the week, with no recognition that more than ten minutes had passed. What I do remember is the week or so of recovery that followed, during which I could barely open my mouth and was almost incapable of drinking, to the extent that my mother threatened a return to the hospital and an intra-venous drip.

With excruciating will, I sipped water, then warm juice through a straw, taking up to an hour to finish a small glass. Each sip hurt my gums, lips, jaw, throat, and head; when my mother brought chicken broth, I could not con-ceive of it making the long, arduous trip down my esoph-agus. Once I had mastered the art of the straw, however, and no longer needed the Percocet, I got hungry, very hungry, which made sense, considering I had gone for ten days with no solid food. The problem was that I still could not fully open my mouth; to do so, and then to close it, caused waves of pain to ripple throughout my body, down to my toes. As soon as I started to consider the pos-sibility of chewing, I returned, every three days, to the dentist to have the cavities cleaned and packed, the pro-cedure causing my head to throb. Worried, my mother brought special treats on a tray, foods she alone knew I loved: bread with almond butter and currant jelly, crème caramel. My grandmother invented a soft chicken terrine with tarragon, a custard so slippery-smooth I could almost drink it, but even as I inhaled the aroma and looked long-ingly, I could not eat; the pain was immense, and the fear of the pain even worse.

It took weeks before I could slide a bite of food between my lips, allow it to soften, then swallow it while trying to freeze the muscles in my face. It was months before I ate toast, popcorn, an apple, anything demanding a serious chew. Sometimes now, twelve years later, I find myself worrying the back of my gums with my tongue, where the hollows from the surgery remain, and clench my jaw involuntarily, remembering—more than the hospital itself, the dentist, the gurney, the Percocet haze—how it felt to be unable to eat.

"I'M HAVING WEIGHT-LOSS SURGERY," ALISON ANNOUNCED into the phone from Boston one morning in the spring of 2000, before I'd had my coffee, when I was still sufficiently tired to think I was dreaming.

"Ha," I said, pinning the phone to my shoulder with my chin and stretching my arms to wake up. I wasn't too sleepy, however, to be surprised that Alison was mentioning weight to me in any context, let alone before 7:00 a.m.; it wasn't a topic we generally discussed in casual conversation.

Alison ignored me. "I'm serious. It's called gastric bypass surgery. Mom and Dad already know."

I had never heard the words *gastric bypass* before, and they sounded cold and clinical. And the very idea of "weight-loss surgery" struck me as insane, even in my daze. If such a thing existed as a legitimate medical procedure, then why weren't all overweight people having it? Maybe this was some kind of a joke. It certainly sounded extreme, and Alison has always been fond of the extreme. Was she talking about a new kind of liposuction? My parents would never agree to that, and although she was old enough to make her own decisions, I was pretty sure that any surgery Alison might have would require their financial assistance, if not full-fledged patronage. Or maybe something was actually wrong with her, something related to weight. Our father had had his gallbladder removed when we were in college, and that had been a pretty serious operation. When I talked to him in the recovery room shortly afterward, for about fifteen minutes, he'd ended the conversation with "Talk to you later, Ali," and I'd thought maybe he was going to die. I couldn't remember him ever confusing the two of us before. Before I could verbalize any questions, however, or even get out of bed, Alison delivered her customary abrupt departure line.

"Got to go, call you later," she announced cheerfully, slamming down the phone. Alison isn't averse to dropping conversational bombs and fleeing the scene. I called my parents.

To my shock, it was true. Alison was scheduled to have gastric bypass surgery in August, just a few months away. It was a legitimate medical procedure, albeit a relatively recent one in its current incarnation. All the doctors our parents and Alison had talked to, including the surgeon who would perform the operation, had pronounced her an ideal candidate.

"But do you think it's a good idea?" I persisted. "You actually think she should do this?" I wanted somebody from whom to take cues. I wasn't yet sure what my stance was, although I knew I needed to have one.

"It was not our decision to make," both our parents said,

which was true. At this point, Alison was nearly thirty years old. Later, though, I wondered about the conversations my parents must have had with each other in private, weighing the risks of major, controversial surgery against what they knew to be Alison's desperate unhappiness with her body, the limitations her obesity, and the self-consciousness and distress it created, placed on her life.

Nobody asked me what I thought, which was actually a good thing, because, for once, I had no idea. Usually I knew what I thought about everything, even if, later on, I realized I had been wrong and had made a fool out of myself in my vehemence. I asked my parents if they had any literature I could borrow on the surgery; sure enough, later in the week I received copies of all the articles my father had managed to gather on gastric bypass surgery. There weren't many, which wasn't surprising, as my father is not much for research and had not, at this point, discovered the Internet. Fortunately, I had.

Gastric bypass is the fastest-growing procedure in the United States. The American Society for Bariatric Surgery estimated that 62,500 operations were performed in the United States in 2002. It is gaining in popularity for a number of reasons, primarily the comprehensive failure of traditional weight-loss methods, including diets and medication. Drugs such as phentermine—the supposedly safe half of the mid-1990s notorious fen-phen—Meridia, and Xenical (which often triggers severe diarrhea)—are waning in popularity because of deaths and subsequent lawsuits, as well as largely unsatisfying results. In middle-stage trials of the most successful obesity drug on the horizon, Regeneron Pharmaceutical's Axokine, patients weighing 220 pounds lost an average of 12.4 pounds in forty-eight weeks. Although the loss of even 10 pounds can have health benefits to the obese, including a 60 percent reduction in the chance of developing diabetes, 12.4 pounds can't sound like much to someone who has more than a hundred to lose.

We can talk all we want to about how obesity is linked to the advent of technology, the introduction of processed food and fast food into the American diet, our sedentary lifestyle, poverty, and an ill-informed public, consisting largely of—if you believe what you see on television—obese men and women looking for someone to blame, suing McDonald's out of desperation. In any event, we have a problem. In 1994 a scientist at Rockefeller University discovered the obesity gene when he noticed that mice lacking it were universally obese. And regardless of whether they carry this gene, human beings have what is called a *set point* for weight. This means that in spite of where we live, what we eat, and how much we exercise, our bodies already have a particular shape in mind. If you spend any time around children, you can see legs that will grow spindly and long, arms already soft and rounded, rib cages distinctly concave. In a group, children's bodies may look the same, but if you examine them individually, you get a glimpse of how these children will evolve, shadowy blueprints of the adults they will become.

⌒

WAS ALISON REALLY A PERFECT CANDIDATE FOR THIS still-controversial surgery, and if so, why? This was what I wanted to know in the beginning, as it was clear Alison planned to go through with the procedure, regardless of what I had to say. The main piece of information that kept cropping up was that gastric bypass was a surgery performed only on the "morbidly obese."

Alison and I have always had a difference of opinion when it comes to how we talk about weight. She herself says *fat* and always has, eschewing the fuzzy euphemisms I prefer, words such as *overweight, large, heavy,* and *big.* (While I agree that *fat* packs more of a punch than any of the synonyms in circulation, it is also one of those words that seem harsh and derogatory when spoken by some-body who isn't using it to describe himself or herself.)

Morbidly obese is another matter altogether. Techni-cally, the phrase describes a person who is at least one hundred pounds over his or her ideal weight, as defined by the National Institutes of Health. We don't use the word *morbid* much in casual conversation, and I under-stand why. To me, it reeks of blood and guts, spectators at the site of a horrific car wreck, even perversity. *Obese,* too, is an ugly word. It sucker-punches all the softness out of *fat,* leaving it distorted and amorphous, gives *morbid* an ugly surface to which to adhere. For some unknown rea-son, *obese* makes me think of Grendel and his monstrous mother. I know it's a medical term and that medical terms are not designed to make people feel better but to clearly identify parts, conditions, and symptoms. Seeing the term over and over, though, as I read up on gastric bypass, I couldn't help feeling manipulated, as though Alison's body were bearing the brunt of the words.

I hadn't realized Alison was morbidly obese. *Morbidly obese* didn't sound like somebody who really wanted to lose weight but was having some trouble; it sounded like somebody with a disease. I was also oblivious to the extent and severity of obesity's health risks. When Alison had been diagnosed with sleep apnea as a result of her weight, I'd looked up the term on-line and learned that the condition can cause brain damage, even death, because of a lack of blood to the brain. I'd experienced a brief resurgence of guilt over my duct-taping days, but to learn that my sister was at significantly higher risk for diabetes, high blood pressure, stroke, heart attack, and almost every type of cancer came as a cruel shock. Alison wasn't yet thirty. If she was at risk for a heart attack now, I didn't even want to think about where she would be thirty years down the line if she didn't lose weight.

Feeling protective and a little scared, I called Alison again, but of course she was out. Alison is generally out. Which was only one of the dozens of reasons I had trouble picturing her under the knife, confined to a hospital room with tubes coming out of her in every direction, liquid dripping into her inert body through a looming IV. (For me, Alison's gastric bypass marked the end of, among other, more significant illusions, the notion that major surgery resembles what happens on *ER*.) Even unhappy or deflated, Alison retains a fierce, defiant quality that made it hard to imagine her helpless and prone. As difficult as it was to imagine her incapacitated, though, it was harder still to conceive of the surgery working.

Over the next couple of days, I kept trying to picture Alison thin. Somehow I couldn't quite do it. I would envision her head propped up on other people's necks and bodies, but the bodies in my visions never exactly matched the head—they were too short or too tall or otherwise out of proportion. Sometimes I would picture her the way she had looked as a child, but blown up, which made for a funhouse image, distorted and poorly proportioned. I thought about calling and asking her if *she* could picture herself thin, or how she thought she would look if the procedure worked, but it seemed insensitive, so I didn't. I keep a picture of the two of us at around ten and eleven above my desk, and if I squinted while staring at it, I could attenuate her image, but the result still didn't look like Alison.

ALISON FIRST LEARNED ABOUT GASTRIC BYPASS SURGERY when she switched over to my mother's primary care physician because of a change in her health insurance policy. One day when my mother was in for a checkup, the doctor mentioned to her that he thought Alison would be a good candidate for a new procedure that was being performed with great success at the Boston University Medical Center, among other area hospitals. The surgery was a significantly updated version of the stomach stapling that had gained notoriety in the 1970s and 1980s, largely due to a number of gruesome, probably preventable deaths. My mother passed on this information to Alison, whose curiosity was piqued, although she did have reservations. Up to that point, Alison had been in the hospital exactly once, to have her tonsils removed, and that experience had been sufficiently traumatic. She had little use for doctors, most of whom were insensitive when discussing her weight and some of whom had been downright rude to her as they bemoaned the national obesity crisis, handed her stacks of useless diet pamphlets, and instructed her to lose weight before her next physical. She had never met a doctor who seemed to care about her or who made her feel as though serious weight loss was a real possibility.

Alison decided to set up an informational interview with the surgeon recommended by her new doctor. The first meeting was conducted by one of the nurses who worked with the surgeon, a specialist whose entire practice consists in performing gastric bypass surgeries. She drove herself to the appointment, followed the nurse into her office, then sat expressionless for the duration, arms folded tightly across her chest, the way you might sit if someone was trying to sell you an obviously dysfunctional car, the way she had always met me in her bedroom when

I'd persuaded her to unlock the door. The nurse showed her a film depicting the procedure in progress and then brought out the big-ticket item: "before and after" pictures, my favorite part of any fashion magazine. I wish I had seen them: the few I found in the course of my research were out of focus and wholly unconvincing, like the ads for weight-loss creams in which the subject is just poorly groomed and sticking out her stomach in the "before" shot. Something in the images spoke to Alison not of fantasy but of an alternate reality, not of fakery but of transformation. When she looked at the "after" shots, she could almost picture herself. When the nurse asked Alison if she was interested in becoming a candidate, she said yes, and asked how soon she could be scheduled for surgery.

Fortunately, legitimate practitioners are prepared for such reactions, and force potential patients to slow things down. The next step was a battery of psychological tests designed to weed out, before they got their hopes up too high, those who would be unable to handle the physical and emotional trauma of the procedure. The questions were pretty transparent. Most seemed centered on feelings of self-worth, although a few, on subjects such as housekeeping habits and dreams, were not quite so overt. When Alison asked the nurse to explain precisely what was being measured in these tests, the nurse replied, simply, "Stability." It was not until she had left the nurse's office and was curled up at home on her couch reading testimonials from the surgeon's former patients that

Alison realized the magnitude of the domino she'd tipped over. Like the "before and after" images, the patient testimonials seemed very real. For the first time, she told herself, believing every word: this could happen for me.

Stability: an interesting word. The connotations come first; is it just me, or is a person described as *stable* usually a little on the dull side? The word pales next to its wild-child sibling descriptors: *spontaneity, unpredictability, eccentricity, creativity, individuality.* Instability, however, is hardly desirable. If you are unstable, you are imbalanced, possibly a little dangerous, inconsistent, unreliable, on the edge. I know there are many people who would beg to differ, my father for one, but in my opinion it's ideal to be a little of both. I thought about contacting a doctor's office and requesting a copy of the psychological screen; I wanted to check out the criteria for stability, now that I knew they existed. If I couldn't imagine what it would be like for Alison to lose twenty pounds, I wondered how a psychiatrist would judge if she was mentally prepared to lose ten times that amount. I wondered if *I* thought she was.

As it turned out, Alison was by far the most calm, ostensibly stable person with whom I discussed her impending surgery. She viewed the gastric bypass as a natural progression in her life—destiny falling into her waiting lap. The people around her, whether or not she realized it, were getting a little hysterical. Several relatives called to tell me they feared for her safety. I reported back that according to my research, and in light of the caliber and experience of her medical team, complica-

THE WEIGHT OF IT 143

tions were extremely unlikely, and treatable if they occurred. A few others expressed both doubt that the surgery would work and concern that its failure would be devastating for Alison. (I kept my mouth shut at this— but what I wanted to say was, "And then what? She'll be obese? Too late! She already is!") Alison was disturbed by the fact that some of her closest friends and loved ones, people who had known her for decades but had stood on the sidelines as she tried and failed to lose weight in almost every possible way, advised against the procedure; and as time went on, so was I. Regardless of how she explained the precautions, the technique, or the follow-up care, nobody seemed to accept the fact that the procedure could actually work.

A friend had the gall to suggest to me that Alison was perhaps looking for an easy way out, and I was so offended I told her I thought we needed to take a little break from speaking to each other. Afterward, though, I kept repeating those words in my head. I knew from taking the easy way out, as my Bubby would have said. I often opted for the shortcut instead of the extra lap, the fabricated lateness excuse rather than an additional few hours of work. In fact, I had always thought of Alison as the workhorse to my lazybones. As a child, I'd paid Alison and Jacy to clean my bedroom, tricked Alison into carrying my library books out to the car. In other words, I didn't walk if I could ride. Alison, on the other hand, could work through the night if the situation required, two nights in an emergency. She could work until her hands calloused, eyelids dropped shut on their own accord. Why, then—although I knew she had to have the surgery, and I wanted her to have it—couldn't I stop thinking that what my friend had said was true? Alison *was* taking the easy way out.

Although I had no way of knowing this in advance, gastric bypass surgery is not an easy way out, any more than remaining obese would have been. It's that old question of the devil you know versus the devil you don't—at first I could not see how brave a decision it was to choose the surgery, that once again Alison was marching straight down the less-traveled path toward a fate of her own choosing. Even our parents, who knew better than anyone else what Alison had endured as a result of her weight, expressed more concern than Alison had anticipated as the date of the surgery neared. They kept asking her if she was *absolutely certain* she wanted to go through with it; obviously, they were worried about the risks and ramifications. But the more everyone cautioned Alison against the procedure, the more she realized that nobody really understood her situation, not even her immediate family. I tried, but I don't think any of us could comprehend what it meant for her to see a way out. This was not a quick fix; rather, it was a valiant last resort.

It didn't really matter what any of us thought, how scared or dubious we were. Alison was a twenty-nine-year-old who had lived in the world as a fat person for her entire adult life. This situation rendered my opinion irrelevant on all weight-related subjects, as Alison herself had told me many times and as I was finally coming to see. As much as I could empathize with Alison, could imagine what it felt like to be her, I could not know what it was like to be fat, which made me speculate on what Alison would think about the quick-fix accusation. Did Alison harbor doubts that the surgery would work? Did she, like me, ever think it sounded too good to be true, a magical cure for an all-too-earthbound reality? As it turns out, Alison worried not that the surgery *wouldn't* work but that it *would*. The nicest thing anybody had said to her in years about her appearance was that she'd be so pretty if she lost weight—which, if you think about it, is a terrible thing to say. And although she recognized the implicit insult, Alison took heart whenever she heard it. It terrified her to imagine people liking her for the wrong reasons, a common concern that had never before been an issue for her.

THE MONTHS LEADING UP TO THE SURGERY WERE ROUGH for Alison, in anticipated and unanticipated ways. The surgeon and her new psychiatrist recommended that she attempt to modify her diet in preparation for the way her eating habits would, by necessity, change after she'd undergone the procedure. She tried to cut down on calories, especially fats and sugary foods, but the knowledge that she would no longer be able to eat more than a small serving of some of her favorite foods postsurgery made her efforts especially difficult. The week before the surgery was the worst of all. She stocked up on all the things she'd been told she wouldn't be able to eat anymore, such as candy and rice and pasta and bread; she ate a lot of sushi that week because she had read that rice was going to be the hardest food to digest postsurgery. She kept thinking: I'll never eat sushi again. This is the last eel roll I'll ever have in my life.

Three days before the surgery, while reviewing her burgeoning file of gastric bypass–related materials (to which I'd contributed some of my findings), Alison noticed something, in a post-op photograph of a patient, that had previously escaped her attention. She called our mother and started to cry so hard she couldn't get the words out. Finally, she managed to explain what was bothering her: she was going to have a scar for the rest of her life. For an hour or so that night she thought she might cancel the surgery. Somehow the sight of the scar—a thick, uneven white slash across the sexless patient's torso—had hit home the enormity of what she had decided to do in a way that nothing or nobody else had managed to. She called the surgeon, who confirmed that she would indeed have a six-inch scar on her stomach and a smaller one where the feeding tube would be. This reminder sent her into another tailspin; she'd forgotten about the feeding tube. I found it surprising that the image of the scar was what finally caused her to panic. What is a scar, after all? It is the memory of a wound, a notch on the belt of your past.

⤚

ON AUGUST 22, 2000, MY PARENTS PICKED UP ALISON AT her Cambridge apartment in the dim predawn and drove her to the hospital where she was scheduled to be rolled in before breakfast time. She was so nervous that she remembers only one conversation from that morning. As she was lying in the hospital bed, one of the assisting surgeons handed her a clipboard with release forms to sign and asked if she would mind authorizing the doctors to remove some fat during the procedure for a study they were doing at the medical school. He explained that scientists were pretty sure that the fat cells in a fat person were actually different from the fat cells in a thin person and that samples were needed for the lab work being conducted to test this hypothesis. Alison looked at the doctor as though he were crazy. "Are you kidding?" she said. "Fat? Take as much as you want."

Of course, the amount of fat removed by the researcher was minute, undetectable postoperation, as Alison knew full well. Gastric bypass is not cosmetic surgery. It is not about removing fat. It is about forcing the body to consume and digest food differently than it has been doing. Because the procedure has long-term ramifications, the decision to perform it—or to have it performed—is not taken lightly. In fact, there are specific, universal criteria used to determine whether a person is a good candidate for gastric bypass surgery, beyond the preliminary psychiatric evaluation. Legitimate surgeons will not perform the procedure on an individual who does not have an extensive, documented history of trying and failing to lose and keep off weight by means of other, noninvasive weight-loss treatments. (For most morbidly obese individuals, meeting this particular requirement is hardly a problem. Nonoperative weight-loss methods are almost never effective for the obese. In fact, the yo-yo dieting most obese people subject themselves to over a lifetime actually slows metabolism and leads to weight *gain*, not loss.) You cannot have a drug or alcohol problem (although you may be considered if you have completed a treatment program and have a year or more of sobriety behind you), and you cannot suffer from any psychological or medical problems that would increase the risks to your health. In general, you must be of sound physical and mental health and receive a nutrition evaluation, the above-mentioned psychological evaluation, and clearance from your medical doctor. The physical evaluation for potential candidates includes a number of tests of heart and lung function, X rays of the stomach and gallbladder, and a complete blood workup. A patient who is already experiencing significant health problems related to morbid obesity is much more likely to have harmful or even fatal repercussions from the procedure and is therefore usually not a candidate. Patients who cannot walk comfortably before the surgery because of cardiopulmonary failure, for example, will not be able to walk comfortably immediately following the surgery; they are therefore at serious risk for blood clots that can travel to the heart and cause death, as well as for pneumonia and pressure sores.

The concept of weight-loss surgery emerged when surgeons performing cancer- or ulcer-related operations that removed portions of the stomach or small intestine began to notice that their patients almost always lost weight after the procedure. The intestinal bypass, performed with some frequency starting in the 1960s, led to weight loss as a result of what is called *malabsorption*. Patients could eat normally and would drop pounds because their bodies could not properly digest food, which passed through the digestive tract so quickly that few calories were absorbed. The side effects, however, were often fatal, as essential nutrients passed through too quickly as well, leading to severe malnutrition.

When we eat, food moves through the digestive tract, and enzymes digest and absorb both calories and nutrients, giving us energy and sustenance. The food moves down the esophagus to the stomach, where acid continues the digestive process, then to the duodenum—the first part of the twenty-foot-long small intestine—where bile and pancreatic juices do their part. It is in the duodenum that most of the calcium and iron we ingest is absorbed. In the rest of the small intestine—the jejunum and the ileum— the digestive process is completed; any food that cannot be digested in the small intestine is stored in the large intestine until it is excreted. Gastric bypass surgery changes the digestive process in two ways. First, a small pouch is created in the stomach to restrict food intake. A normal-size stomach can hold about three pints—a fist-size amount—of food. The stomach pouch can hold several tablespoons, two fingers' worth. Second, a Y-shaped section of the small intestine is rerouted and attached to the newly formed stomach pouch so that food bypasses the lower stomach, the duodenum, and the first portion of the jejunum altogether, reducing the amount of calories and nutrients (which must be taken as supplements, sometimes in the form of injections) absorbed by the body. Patients who undergo this procedure—the most effective of the types available—usually lose at least two thirds of their excess weight within two years.

Success does not come cheap. Gastric bypass surgery costs an average of $15,000, and that figure does not include subsequent procedures to remove unsightly skin flaps resulting from rapid weight loss. But the surgery is an attractive option to an insurance industry waking up to the fact that obesity is appallingly expensive. In 2003 the American Obesity Association estimated obesity's costs at $100 billion; also in 2003, Reuters reported that companies are spending $12 billion annually on obesity-related conditions. Many experts believe obesity is now the nation's biggest health problem, replacing familiar demons: a 2002 study by Roland Sturm of the RAND Corporation determined that obesity has a "stronger association with the occurrence of chronic medical conditions, reduced physical health-related quality of life and increased health care and medication expenditures than smoking or problem drinking." A 1999 analysis in the *Journal of the American Medical Association* put the number of adult obesity deaths at 280,000 to 325,000 annually. Today, almost half a million people in this country are dying—*dying*—each year from being too fat.

While the risks are real if statistically minute and the procedure is controversial, the long-term health benefits are remarkable. After a gastric bypass, most patients emerge free of diabetes and hypertension and with drastically reduced occurrences of sleep apnea, arthritis, and other health problems, including degenerative, inordinately expensive-to-treat conditions such as cancer and heart disease, the bane of insurance companies' existence. A patient who has undergone the procedure, in other words, is almost guaranteed to require fewer visits to doctors or hospitals and significantly less medication and/or surgery over a lifetime. Depending on the patient's insurance policy, obtaining preauthorization for a gastric bypass can take as little as two weeks, and most experts speculate that those companies that don't pay for the procedure now will soon do so—it is that cost-effective.

Gastric bypass is considered major, invasive surgery and usually requires a hospital stay of at least a couple of days for recovery from the anesthesia and overall trauma, in addition to the fact that initially the patient is unable to eat and requires an IV. It took Alison, a chef at one of Boston's top catering companies, several months before she could resume anything approximating a normal diet, although she was out of the hospital in a week. For the first two weeks or so, she consumed only beverages; when her stomach and intestine started to heal, she graduated to foods puréed in the blender, including a tuna shake described to me in graphic detail, but she abstained from sugar and fat, which initially made her sick in even minuscule portions. I had read patient testimonials in which formerly obese people claimed dissatisfaction with their gastric bypass surgeries because they were no longer able to eat more than a spoonful of food at a time. I knew Alison had feared this possibility, too. Now, three years after her surgery, Alison eats about the same amount and kinds of food as many women I know—which is to say like a thirty-two-year-old who enjoys eating but tries not to overindulge.

Of course, for the first time in her life, Alison is not really watching her weight; she doesn't have to. There are documented cases in which people have had gastric bypass surgery, lost the intended weight, and then gradually regained all of it, but they are far and few between, and you almost have to work at it to eat enough to make this a possibility. There are a million issues, however, for Alison regarding her new relationship to food and to her own body. For one thing, as a chef who has always worked with and enjoyed rich ingredients, what does it mean to spend each day surrounded by foods she cannot eat? For another, how does it feel to walk out the door each morning in the body she has dreamed of since childhood? I can't answer those questions; they are Alison's to grapple with. My story is this: in a matter of months my other half, the person on the planet to whom I am most closely tied, shed her old body as a snake sheds its skin and emerged with a different one, leaving me reeling and desperate to find meaning in the change. It is an age-old question, boiled down to nearly two hundred pounds of excess flesh: How and why do we become the people we are?

S I X

rebirth

The first time I saw Alison after the surgery, she looked . . . exactly the same. At least I thought she did when I saw her walking down the ramp off the boat from Woods Hole, as I waited with my dad to bring her back to the house on Martha's Vineyard.

"She looks great, don't you think?" my dad elbowed me, his eyes following Alison, who had somehow managed, in spite of being stitched up the middle, to lug three enormous duffle bags and a mysterious package all the way from Boston by herself for a three-day stay. To me she looked exactly like Alison. When she got close enough, she handed my dad the biggest two bags and me the smallest one. She was wearing new sunglasses with green

lenses, and immediately I decided that I would get sunglasses with green lenses, too.

"Aren't you going to say how great I look even though
I'm still in recovery?" she asked me as I buckled under the
weight of the bag. My dad was red-faced and breathing
hard just ahead of us under his share of the load. Before I
could respond, she looked around at my dad and then
leaned in closer to me. "I'll show you my stitches when
we get there," she stage-whispered. "Dad will get mad if I
do it now." I refrained from pointing out that the Vineyard Haven police might also get mad if Alison removed
her sundress in the middle of the A & P parking lot.
Under other circumstances I would have been curious to
see the stitches. I have an iron stomach and a fascination
for graphic medical imagery. However, I feared (justifi-
ably) that I would soon be getting not just a close-up and
personal viewing of the stitches but a whole lot of other
information I would have preferred to read about in a
medical journal, if at all, and not while I was spreading
butter on my corn on the cob. As she sped up and started
talking to our dad, I fell back and studied her, her step
light and assured now that we were carrying all her
things.

She *did* look the same, which didn't surprise me when
I stopped to think about it, considering she was theoretically going to lose weight over the course of a year or
more and not in the first two weeks out of the hospital.
Her hair, which had been white blonde for a year or so,
was long and straight. Her skin was smooth and unlined,

childlike, as a result of the fifteen years she'd spent out of the sun. It occurred to me that she might actually go to the beach, but that was too much to fathom. The last time Alison had been on Lambert's Cove, she'd been wearing a long black skirt and a sweater and had fallen asleep on her back with a newspaper over her head for a few hours until we woke her up to leave, her exposed feet and ankles glowing bright red in the late afternoon dimness.

Later that day we drove into town for dinner, and Alison and I walked up and down Main Street, where we used to get all our back-to-school clothes. I found myself thinking how normal it seemed to be walking this particular route with Alison, how I knew which stores she would want to go into, what she would covet.

"Maybe I'll buy some clothes there next year," Alison said, as we walked out of one store she had determined carried nothing that would look good on me.

"Maybe you will," I said, feeling indulgent and hopeful myself. When I spotted my father hiding around a corner and spying on us, waiting for one of us to catch sight of him, the circle was complete—it could have been twenty years ago, easy, even more so when my mother, holding my grandmother's arm, passed us on the sidewalk and spotted my father, too, still peering around the corner with a Cheshire cat grin.

"Come on, Joel. Grow up," she said, and Mormor winked at us. At dinner I noticed that although Alison still appeared unchanged, the rest of us seemed somehow lighter. That first meal, I forced myself not to watch while she ate, but she ate next to nothing. She sipped at a glass of water and inquired after our meals, criticizing one piece of fish as looking overcooked and complimenting the almond crust on another, but she didn't eat much beyond some clam chowder broth and the soft innards of a piece of bread. She did attempt to launch into a description of some of the side effects she was experiencing as a result of the surgery, such as the aptly named "dumping syndrome," but one look from my mother put a quick end to that subject. When Alison and her entourage of luggage left the island a few days later, I found myself remembering her stay as a dream. It hadn't seemed real somehow, that she had been there; it had been so long since somebody had begged me to look at photos, run an errand, or rent a movie in a way that implied my presence was essential to the success of the experience that I found myself feeling flattered instead of exasperated.

PREVIOUSLY I DESCRIBED FATNESS AS AN EXTREME STATE, reached so gradually that it sneaks up on you. As it turns out, thinness has the same quality. In the late spring of the year after Alison's surgery, we took our first real family vacation in over a decade. The rest of us had traveled together during that time, but Alison had spent her breaks with friends or stopped by on Martha's Vineyard for a day or two, close enough to her home in Boston that she could always go back if she wanted or needed to. This time there would be no abrupt departures. We were headed for North Captiva, a tiny place with no cars, no industry other than a closet-size food mart, and fewer than a hundred people in residence on any given day. This vacation was notable for a handful of reasons, aside from the fact that it happened at all and in such a remote and secluded location. For one, it was the first time I can remember seeing my sister in a bathing suit as an adult; she had usually worn a giant T-shirt down to her knees at the beach. For another, it was the only time since elementary school that I remember her hounding us to make sure she was in every photograph, even the nature shots.

As soon as we arrived at the house, Alison invited me into her little room to watch her unpack. Her room at this house was as small as the room she'd had in my parents' first house, the one in which she'd kept sneaking out of her crib. Alison, furious about the room situation, did not agree that it was reasonable for Ben and me to have the larger room, which slept two, for the duration of the stay.

"It's not *my* fault you got married," she said upon viewing the discrepancy. It was a good thing there were more important matters to occupy our attention, such as her wardrobe.

Although I'd expected that even if she lost only a small amount of weight, Alison would be revamping her wardrobe, I was astonished at what she had managed to purchase after losing nearly a hundred pounds. I sat on the floor by the bed as she held up each new piece of clothing, shaking it out, placing it over her body like a paper doll to give me an idea of what it would look like on her, and then folded it carefully in a pile of similar items. As blouse after wrap after skirt was unfurled, I became uncomfortably aware that I had brought four pairs of shorts and a handful of T-shirts on this trip, along with my favorite bathing suit, whose feelings were never hurt when my mother asked after its saggy bottom and frayed elastic each year. As if she sensed what I was thinking, Alison stopped mid-shake of what was possibly a pair of gauzy harem pants and looked at me with more than a little pity.

"You can borrow some of this stuff if you need to," she said. I didn't point out that a wardrobe change was probably unnecessary for the big viewing of *Deerhunter* my father had planned for that evening. Somehow I knew there would be time later on to tease her. Somehow I knew she'd been waiting a long time to be able to say what she'd just said.

The first full day of the trip I found myself watching Alison almost as if she were in a movie. I narrated her actions in my head, adding well-earned exclamation points: "There's Alison putting on shorts. Shorts! There's Alison in a tank top, not as an undershirt but to wear on its own! There's Alison showing my mother a new pink sweater. Did I just say pink?!" My eyes were drawn to her as though she were in color and the rest of us in black and white—and not just because she had so much more energy. A New Yorker in spirit if not in residence, Alison has worn black from head to toe forever, down to year-round, heavy, high-heeled boots. The boots were nowhere in sight. All week she emerged from her bedroom in summery, tropical-hued ensembles: aqua shirts with lime green skirts and fuchsia flip-flops, lemon yellow shirts and madras shorts, the likes of which I'd seen only in rare college photographs of our mom. Even the bathing suit was raspberry red. The old uniform had apparently been scrapped, except at work, where she had to wear the standard-issue black pants and white coat. It made me smile to picture her shopping for all these new clothes.

All week I kept watching her—on the island she was a butterfly in a cage—and if she noticed, I don't think she minded. It was a far cry from the days when her eyes had barely left our faces in an aggressive attempt to catch us watching her critically. Everywhere we went she commented on who had said hello to her, who had waved, who had checked her out as she walked to the soda machine; and she wasn't exaggerating: I was watching other people watch her, too. In my unremarkable getups and winter-dull hair, I was the stepsister to her platinum blonde, bejeweled Cinderella, and her delight in the attention she received was a marvel to behold. I think she wanted me to be envious, and I was, but maybe not quite in the way she imagined. How in less than nine months had she acquired that confident swagger, a more polished, solid version of her youthful panache? She still had a lot of weight to lose, at least another hundred pounds, but instead of seeming daunted, she exuded a powerful self-awareness, a defiant pride. That week I paid a lot of attention to my own body. I noticed the knobs on the outer edges of my wrists, the muscles that spread when my calves lay flat on the deck. It was as though I, too, was discovering a physical self that felt like a stranger's; her awareness seemed somehow contagious.

Each morning and afternoon Alison walked for miles up and down the beach with my mother looking for shells, as she had as a child. And I took up my childhood role, lying on the beach reading as they walked, my father beside me with his book and a highlighter pen. Alison must have walked more in that week than in the previous two decades combined. She drove the golf cart, the island's only means of transportation, with one tanned hand on the steering wheel, sunglass-sheltered eyes on the path ahead; my eyes remained on her altered-but-still-recognizable profile. She ate, too, and although certainly more than the ominous tablespoonful of food described in the gastric bypass literature, much, much less than in the past—no full-size bags of chips after an enormous dinner, no half-gallon cartons of ice cream early in the morning. Just meals, like the rest of us, maybe a Popsicle in the afternoon, a cookie or two after one of those long walks on the beach.

Back home in cold, gray New York, I opened my mailbox one day to find that my father had sent copies of his photos from the trip. I filtered out the fuzzy, headless, or red-eyed rejects (we are creative in my family, but we can't take pictures) and spread out the remaining images on my coffee table. Two in particular caught my eye. The first was a close-up of my head and Alison's, both of us sunburned, both wearing braids, as we always had as little girls. It had been taken on the last day of the trip. We'd been waiting in the hot sun for the boat that would take us back to the mainland, when suddenly my dad broke the silence.

"Sandra, do you think Amy and Alison look anything alike?" he said, and immediately Alison and I looked at each other.

"Don't look so flattered," Alison said quickly, sarcastically, and I was so taken aback by the flash of defensiveness that I didn't know what to say.

"Are you kidding me?" my mother said, also a little angry, but at my dad. "Give me the camera." I didn't need to see the picture to know I agreed with my mom, but there it was: proof. I wondered whether the days of being mistaken for twins were returning. I wondered how that would make Alison feel. I thought it felt pretty good.

The other picture I liked was of Alison standing alone on the beach. She was wearing one of her new bright outfits, layered pink-and-peach stretchy tank tops and a swirly-patterned skirt—she looked like a psychedelic tequila sunrise, her blonde hair shining in the waning light in front of a glistening green sea. On the last night of the trip, when we were packing to go home, I had finally felt comfortable asking her why all her new clothes were so colorful. I half expected her to think I was mocking her and to fire back an insult about my family of khakis, but she took me seriously, so seriously that I knew she'd been thinking about this a lot on her own. In fact, she answered as though I were a stranger interviewing her, not just her messy sister sprawled on the floor of her bedroom while our mother packed sand dollars in empty cans out on the deck and our father watched the ending of *The Sixth Sense* for the fourth time in the living room, still trying to figure it out.

"For my whole life I've been hiding my body in dark shapeless clothes," she said. "I decided it was time to celebrate. Finally, I have nothing to hide."

PEOPLE ARE AS INTERESTED IN A WEIGHT-LOSS SUCCESS story as they are uninterested in a fat person. Six months later, when I told my friends that Alison was coming to New York for a weekend, everyone wanted to see her. It's not fair to imply that my friends had not been interested in Alison before she lost weight. Still, I wasn't expecting quite the level of interest this visit attracted, and I asked Alison what to do.

"It's a curse, Amy, being so popular," she sighed, and even though I was alone in my apartment at the time, I rolled my eyes.

"Is there anybody you feel strongly about seeing?" I asked, ignoring the comment.

"Seeing?" she said. "It's not about seeing, it's about being *seen*. We'll have a dinner party. I'll cook. And don't worry. We'll find you something to wear."

Even now, three years after her surgery, people are

always asking me what they should say to Alison when they see her. I have received anxious late-night phone calls from friends who ran into her and worried she'd been offended when they told her how great she looked; I've received equally anxious calls from friends who wanted to make sure it had been the right choice not to say anything, as they didn't want Alison to think they hadn't thought she looked great before. I sympathize with people who don't know how to react to such a dramatic change in appearance, as I am often in situations where I don't know just what to say. In this case, however, there is only one proper reaction: Alison, you look great. If you don't say it, she will, or else she will call me as soon as you leave to ask me what's wrong with you and to suggest that maybe you should get your vision checked and to imply that maybe, just maybe, you're a teensy bit rude. Don't get me wrong; I am hardly trying to scrounge up compliments on Alison's behalf, although I should say here, or she will hound me for years, that she does indeed look amazing and that even though I have told her this a hundred times, it will never quite be enough. To be honest, I find this a little distasteful, the incessant need for praise and affirmation, although I know this makes me sound Scrooge-like and uptight. Again in the name of honesty, and in spite of my heartfelt love for her natural exuberance, I confess to wishing, on occasion, that Alison would approach her new body a little less like a drag queen at life's penultimate cabaret.

On some level, now that Alison is thin and has no need

to be angry at the world or to act out to command the attention she deserves, do I wish she would tone down her theatrics? I force myself to think about this for a while. I, for one, don't believe that weight informs personality, but I do believe it can *mask* personality, throw certain aspects of it under a spotlight, subdue and smooth out others as surely as a metal file. Alison was flamboyant long before she was fat, and when she wasn't, she seemed least like herself. If now she lowered her head modestly, waiting for praise that sometimes came and sometimes didn't, if she strove for understatement, made herself invisible so as to deflect stares instead of soliciting them, she would be another person altogether, and I would be without the other half of myself—for Alison's existence is the yang to my yin, and we each enable the other to swirl around to the other side when we need to, because we, more so than anybody else, see that capacity in each other. If her newfound body gives her additional confidence and throws those traits that have been most dramatically repressed into focus, then I will accept them and try even to celebrate them—although I would prefer that any temptation to raise herself out of a sunroof, along with flashing of all kinds, be kept to a minimum when I am around.

When Alison arrived at my apartment on the morning of the dinner party she'd asked me to arrange, she was ready to shop: both for food and for an outfit in which to wow the guests. After a trip to Fairway, my favorite grocery store and one of the places Alison likes to visit when she's in town, we headed to H & M, a Swedish clothing emporium we'd visited on the ill-fated clog trip to Sweden and that had recently opened a branch in New York. The clothes are trendy and cheap, and there are a lot of them, making it a perfect spot to buy an outfit you may wear only once, in my case; and if you are Alison, a perfect spot to buy seventeen outfits you will wear all the time but can't really afford and may have to beg your sister to lend you some money for—making the thirty people behind you in line pretty angry by carrying out the negotiations just as you get to the cash register.

As we walked up Fifth Avenue, past store windows featuring those plastic models with attenuated limbs that remind me of praying mantises, it occurred to me that this was the first time Alison and I had gone clothes shopping together, on equal footing, since we had opened our own bank accounts. I wondered what shopping with Alison would feel like now that she could buy the clothes she wanted to buy, the ones she'd sometimes bought anyway and let hang in the back of her closet. I wondered if she would ask me what I thought of her choices and if I would be able to say things like "Well, I think it's a little low cut for a christening, but if you want your cleavage to remind the other guests of the baby's nursing mother, then I guess it's all right."

As soon as we walked into the store, I wanted to leave. The first floor was packed with what seemed like hundreds of people, tourists speaking a dozen different languages, natives on Saturday shopping sprees bearing bags from Daffy's and Century 21. I looked at Alison to gauge her reaction, but she was surveying the scene as if she'd randomly stepped off the sidewalk and into the Emerald City.

"This is amazing," she breathed, and I felt my shoulders lower, my jaw unclench. I was not going to ruin this for her; I liked shopping, and I could put up with a crowd scene, even if it resembled the Gallipoli battlefield and even if I had ten people coming for dinner in a scant five hours and needed to clean the apartment, walk the dog, shower, and dress. Alison had to cook most of the meal, in an unfamiliar kitchen, and I suspected there were ingredients we still needed to buy, but these considerations did not appear to concern her. Before I could answer, she was off and running; the next time I saw her, I couldn't actually see her: the pile of clothes in her arms was substantially higher than her head.

"Hey, Amo," she said. "I'm just going to try on a few things. Okay?" The one skirt I'd found I put on the end of the nearest rack. I didn't need a new skirt, anyway, and if I avoided the line at the dressing room that snaked out onto the sidewalk, I could wait in the cash register line for Alison if—as seemed likely—she found anything she wanted to buy. In a miracle of calisthenics and contortion, Alison's hand managed to eke out a space in the pile. With her index and third fingers she clipped onto the skirt I'd just discarded.

"This is cute," she mused. "Do you think they have my size?"

"Do you have your checkbook?" I countered, feeling benevolence leak out of me and pool on the floor at my feet.

"I'll be back in a few minutes," my little master of understatement informed me, stomping off to the extent a person can stomp under the weight of a five-foot heap of Swedish halter tops and boot-cut jeans. Three hours later, as we left the store in mutual anger, it occurred to me that Alison had not asked me to come into the dressing room with her to help her decide what to buy. This was not out of modesty; I think I have established that you, too, can probably see Alison's surgery scars if you ask nicely. It was not that I'd been holding a spot in line for her; after reaching the head of the line three times with no sign of Alison, I'd given up and joined the glazed-eyed men sitting on benches at the front of the store, reading the newspaper until female or, occasionally, male companions joined them at the front door with smiles and full H & M bags. I wanted to ask her why, but I felt foolish doing so. It would make me seem whiny and pathetic, and I wasn't in the mood to have my taste insulted, if that was the card she was going to play. After a few minutes of walking in silence, though, I suddenly didn't feel mad anymore.

"Ali?" I ventured.

"Yeah?" she answered suspiciously, although I could

tell she wasn't mad anymore either. I forced myself to think of the stash of old jeans Alison had kept for so long in her closet, jeans she would say she was "saving," whenever it was gently suggested they join the bags of clothes headed for the donation box in the center of town.

"What are you wearing tonight?" I said.

Half an hour before the guests were to arrive, Alison had most of the food preparation under control. Her individual molten chocolate cakes were in the freezer, ready for baking; the raspberry purée she'd brought from Boston was in a squeeze bottle in the refrigerator. We were also having beef tenderloin; a salad with pine nuts, because Alison remembered that one of my friends especially liked them; crispy risotto cakes; a sweet potato purée; and "passed hors d'oeuvres," although I wasn't sure who was going to be doing the passing—besides, a person holding a tray in the middle of my living room could be reached by all those present, without anyone having to pass.

Now, to my secret gratification, she showed me her new clothes. The way she lay them out on the floor and couch in possible combinations reminded me of how my cousin Mia, at fourteen, had done the same thing earlier that year. It made me realize that, in many ways, Alison was getting a chance to do over adolescence, the way most people I knew wished they could—with the hindsight of an adult perspective and the body she wished she'd had then. A few minutes later, she stood in front of my biggest mirror, tugging at one of her new skirts.

"It looks great," I said. "Stop pulling at it."

"It's still a little too small," she said. "I look lumpy." Excited to offer a solution, I told her to hang on for a second and came back with one of my supertight stretchy slips, the kind I wear under skirts or dresses if I'm not wearing stockings.

"Try this," I said, handing it to her, and she held it up as though it were a bona fide corset. "Come on," I wheedled. "You'll see. It'll work." I went into the kitchen to check on the food, and when I came back, Alison held out the slip, scrunched into a ball.

"I tried it on," she said.

"And?" I prodded.

"It's incredibly uncomfortable and I think it's weird that you wear it," she said. "You don't even need it, and it hurts."

It seemed so simple and obvious coming from Alison: why would I wear voluntarily something uncomfortable, especially something nobody would see? And then this question followed: Why would I wear something to make myself look thinner if I was satisfied with my body as it was? I had to face facts: there was a part of me, assertions to the contrary notwithstanding, that did buy into the thinness rules, that couldn't fight the desire to appear as slim as possible. I took off my own stretchy slip, feeling sheepish and even a little ashamed. That evening I looked around at a group of my closest friends eating beef tenderloin and raving about the crispy risotto cakes. Nobody was paying much attention to me, which was fine, as it was Alison's night all around, a sort of coming-out party, if you will. I had decided to wear my favorite cords and to "pass" the hors d'oeuvres. Alison wore her new skirt, and I didn't see her tug at it once.

IN THE WINTER OF 2003, ALISON SHOWED UP IN NEW York, on my doorstep, one Sunday, swearing she had told me she was coming, although I couldn't remember a confirming call in the previous weeks. It was the first time she'd been back to visit me in two years, since the dinner party she'd catered after the H & M fiasco, which I now refer to as the day I lost all feeling in my feet. It was also the day before what was predicted to be the worst snowstorm in a decade, and I asked Alison how long she was planning to stay. I was already worried about Ben's travel arrangements; he had gone to visit his grandmother in Illinois and was due back the following day.

"I'm only staying for twenty-four hours," she threatened, as if to say, "So you'd better condense all your hostessing skills as best you can." I waited, counting the seconds in my head, for what I knew would come next: "So, where are we going to eat?"

As mentioned before, everything I had read about gastric bypass surgery had led me to believe that formerly obese patients emerged with stomachs so small and compromised that for the rest of their lives they could only nibble at tiny portions of healthful foods. While Alison's surgery has certainly forced her to cut back on the amount she consumes, it does not seem to have prevented her from enjoying food. In spite of her rerouted intestine and diminished stomach pouch, in fact, I sometimes find myself concerned that Alison will eat too much. This concern has led to an equally unexpected return to the days of watching her eat, willing her, in my head, to stop.

Sometimes, when we were teenagers, I would sit next to my sister on the couch or in a movie theater, listening with one ear to the movie, the other to Alison working her way through a bag of popcorn. The compulsive rhythm of the process—the crinkle of the hand in the bag, the chewing, the crinkle, the chewing—made me increasingly tense, until I would hold my hands together tightly in my lap to keep from snatching the bag and hurling it under the seat. Her technique seemed different from mine, although of course it sounded the same. What was different was the fact that even if I ordered a small bag, about halfway through I would stop, wipe my hands on a napkin, and switch to my drink. Even if I finished the bag later on, I never felt compelled to do so; if I was hungry, I would eat it; if not, I wouldn't. With Alison, I was always waiting to see if she would reach the point when she, too, would stop, set aside the bag, at least temporarily, but she never did. She would always work her way through to the bottom, her hand moving unthinkingly in its unceasing round from bag to mouth, until only crumbs and unpopped kernels remained.

The night of Alison's visit, it started to snow, and we

were both too tired to trek out anywhere for dinner. The next morning, when we woke up, the city appeared white from my sixteenth-floor window. I opened the big windows in my living room and we stood by them, listening to how quiet it was outside. We put on coats and boots and ventured out, but it was snowing so hard that nothing was open, and after a few hours of wending through snowdrifts, we returned home exhilarated, feet and hair wet, with some snacks Alison had picked up at the drugstore.

It was clear she could not go back to Boston that night, as planned; in fact, it was clear we weren't going more than a few blocks from the apartment unless one of us was in secret possession of two pairs of cross-country skis. I called Nicole and Ann to see if they wanted to join us for dinner at the French restaurant across the street, and we arranged to meet in a few hours. As I put on water for tea in the kitchen, I could hear Alison rustling through her drugstore bags. By the time I brought her a mug and sat down beside her on the couch a few minutes later, she was a third of the way through a can of salt-and-vinegar Pringles.

"We're meeting Nicole and Ann at eight," I said. "For *dinner.*"

"That's good," she said, tilting the can toward me.

"No thanks," I said, mad at myself for caring, for what I was about to say. "I want to have room for dinner." As she worked on the can, I wondered, and not for the first time, if this was a cause and effect reaction that always produced the undesired effect. I'd seen it happen so many times in the past with Alison. When she was told, warned, cautioned, scolded, or reminded not to eat, she became defensive and defiant. I wasn't sure she ate more in such circumstances, but she certainly didn't set aside the food in question and thank the hall monitor for his or her concern. What really baffled me was why, when I knew that badgering her didn't work and might even be making the situation worse, I couldn't keep myself from admonishing or drawing attention to her overeating. I knew it was possible to avoid criticizing. My mother, for one, has never chastised her. I know this because I have never seen her do so, and because Alison has told me so, many times, every time she catches me watching her eat. I didn't say anything else about the Pringles, and soon it was time to leave. I was glad we wouldn't be eating alone.

At the restaurant I was pretty quiet. The waiter brought us menus, and Alison peered at me over the top of hers, then looked down immediately when she caught my eye.

"I'm not that hungry," she said, setting down her menu after a minute or two. "Do you want to share something, Amo?" I took this as the concession it was, or at least as a kind of explanation. I was too old, it was too late—I could not make Alison thin when we were younger, and I could not make her stay thin now. Alison knew this better than I did; she needed for me to know it, too. She would eat what she ate whether or not I approved, regardless of statistics I quoted from health care journals or patient testimonials, in my presence or when I wasn't around. She had made

the most difficult choice of her life, to seek medical inter-
vention for a problem she could not solve with desire and
willpower, and she deserved to live with the ramifications
of that decision, for better and worse. She deserved—as
we all do, and need to—to make her own mistakes.

After dinner, and a dessert split four ways, we said our
good-byes outside the restaurant. It was snowing even
more heavily than it had been earlier, and I wondered
how long Alison would be stranded in my apartment. The
streets had still not been plowed—I had never seen New
York like this before. My stretch of Columbus Avenue
looked like our front yard in Sudbury during the blizzard
of '78, when my father pulled us to the grocery store on a
sled, an analogy enhanced by the fact that a man across
the street from the restaurant was actually pulling a sled,
on which two toddlers sat train-style, the one in back
holding the one in front around the waist.

"What does that remind you of?" Alison asked.

"I was just thinking the exact same thing," I said. We
were walking straight down the middle of the street.
Beside me, Alison's cheeks were flushed pink from the
cold. The hat she'd called her "hip-hop hat" was covered
with a light layer of snow, as were the shoulders of her
new coral-colored coat. It was slow going, and for a few
minutes we just walked, lifting our boots out of the soft
snow and placing them down again carefully. It was so
quiet I could hear her breathing, and unconsciously I
made mine match.

When we reached my building, we both stopped out-

side under the awning, as though by unspoken agree-
ment. I felt her arm on mine as she leaned ever so slightly
into me. On both sides of the street the cars were completely covered with snow; they could have been haystacks
or piles of logs, if not for the tall buildings behind them,
the man sorting and tying roses in the window of the
laundromat, where one elderly woman stood shaking out
a faded pink sheet. I looked up, and snow fell into my
eyes.

"Ali?" I said without moving my head.

"I'm here," she said, her voice hushed, and I knew she
was taking in the silent white street, the steady snowfall
through which she was viewing it. We'd trudged through
a lot of snow together, but never quite like this. For a few
more seconds, before we turned to go in, I just listened to
her breathe, watching the snow cover build up layers like
paint on soft wood.

A FEW YEARS AGO I CAREFULLY CUT OUT A CARTOON
from the *New Yorker* and affixed it to my refrigerator with
a tiny magnet, where I considered it inconspicuous, surrounded as it was by a photograph of my mother wearing
a lei and careening on a fake windsurfer (taken at a New
England principals' conference) and one of my father
presenting a piece of the famous Boston Garden floor to
"Easy Ed" Macauley, an honor bestowed upon the most
loyal season-ticket holders of my hometown Boston Celtics.
Sometimes I wonder why I put up the cartoon at all, as it

speaks to what I believe is my own worst personality trait and makes me feel a little curdled every time I read it, which is almost every day. The drawing is of two women standing in an abstract rendition of a store. One of the women is pointing at an object on the wall, and the caption reads, "You always think this is going to be the sconce that changes everything for you."

Now, while for me this cartoon sends its clarion call through a bullhorn, I know it does not speak to everyone. Many of my friends and relatives have pointed to it and asked, "Hey, what's up with that cartoon? It's not funny." I agree. It's not funny to spend your life thinking that each goal you set for yourself, just out of reach, will be, if achieved, the one accomplishment or success that will enable you to have what you want—which is, of course, total happiness, peace of mind, and fulfillment. It's especially not funny on those rare days when you actually achieve the goal and realize that you'd been wrong, misled yourself again, that it wasn't *that* goal you needed to reach but another one, just out of reach. If this cartoon speaks to you, then you, too, must sometimes feel like Wile E. Coyote watching the roadrunner inflate himself after being run over by a Mack truck and then run off again, making that infernal *meep, meep* sound that has to haunt Wile E.'s nightmares. I hope I am not burying the moral of the story here, or *a* moral anyway, but perhaps the most personally relevant lesson I have learned from my sister is that the sconce you've eyed and saved up for won't, once acquired, give you everything you've ever wanted, and if you expect it to, you are damned to disappointment. If, however, you can hang that sconce on your wall so it looks beautiful, put a candle in it, and allow it to cast a glow on its corner of the room, a glow in which you can sit and read or think, and not a glow you expect to make the whole room bright enough for everything that will happen in it, that sconce can help you acquire other sconces, patiently and over time, until the light they cast together will be all the light you will need.

I always felt that Alison was waiting until she was thin to start her life, treading water as she listened for an elusive start gun I came to think would never go off. It was not until she actually was thin, though, that I could sympathize with that notion or even begin to question the origins of her point of view, in spite of the fact that I was guilty, in different ways, of holding an identical set of beliefs. We're told, from as early as we can understand language, that it doesn't matter what we look like, that it's what's inside that counts. Some of us will never know that this is a lie. Thanks to Alison, I do. The way we look on the outside informs how others perceive and treat us from the very start. It's naive to deny that we reflect what and who society tells us we are. Sure, Alison at 317 pounds is the same person as Alison at 120; either way, she is made up of the same one-of-a-kind mix of genes and experience. But as I watch her walk differently, talk differently, *think* differently in her new body, sometimes it's hard to remember.

Alison *is* starting her life again, in a way. I see that now, and these days it doesn't make me sad, just a little angry. And yet in a way, I get to start over, too, for I have learned many things from my sister about how to live, including the necessity of carving out a space for yourself whatever its size and shape, and living as empathetically, emphatically, and largely as you possibly can.

SEVEN

wonderland

In November 2002, my parents turned sixty, and Alison and I decided to throw them a birthday party—not just a birthday party but the birthday party to end all birthday parties, my blind ambition and Alison's foolhardy grandiosity wrapped into one exhausting extravaganza, with 120 guests invited, most of whom RSVP'ed yes. In spite of my weekly pleas that we make it a potluck, Alison refused to budge from her announcement, early on, that she was going to plan the menu, purchase or rent all the food, beverages, table linens, and flowers, and prepare everything herself.

"Don't worry," she kept assuring me. "I won't let things get out of control." This I knew to be a lie, although I was less concerned that she would overwork herself—I had taken on the remaining party-related responsibilities—and more concerned that I would be presented, after the fact, with a bill for two hundred two-pound lobsters and forty-five bottles of Veuve Clicquot. As the date of the party approached, I kept calling Alison just to check in. Although I hated how much I sounded like our father, I found myself saying things like "It will be a real disaster if all those people have nothing to eat" and "Some of these people are driving all day to get here—they're going to need a real dinner when they arrive." By the week before the party, Alison had stopped returning my phone calls altogether.

On my way to Sudbury on the morning of the party, I picked up two large cakes to bring, just in case they were needed, along with the food I had been able to make the evening before, which wasn't much. I had lined up Mormor for as many deviled eggs as she could handle, and both of my aunts and my best friend's mother had promised contributions. All this, however—even if Mormor went to town with the eggs—would not be enough for a fraction of the guests as a snack, let alone a meal. I pulled up in the First Parish church parking lot, the same church where Alison had held court under the horse chestnut tree on the front lawn as an eight-year-old and whose main building we'd rented for the evening's events. Alison was sitting on the roof of the car, and I could tell from a distance of thirty feet that she hadn't slept the night before. As I neared, she leaped down and removed her sunglasses, regarding me through narrowed eyes, ready to snap.

"What are you doing out here?" I asked, trying not to pick a fight before we'd so much as begun. As the one who lived in the same state as the church, Alison had promised to make the arrangements for getting the key.

"Don't start," she said. "Follow me. I think one of those windows might be unlocked." Our party preparations began thus, with me hoisting up Alison to break into a church, in plain sight of three roads and who knows how many Sudbury police officers? When she let me in through the back door, I gave her a look. This was not my idea of an auspicious launch.

"What?" she said, countering with a look of her own. "We're in, aren't we?"

"I just wish we hadn't had to do it that way," I said, remembering to breathe and keep my voice even, a New Year's resolution I'd made one year for all future dealings with Alison.

"Oh, me, too," she said, relaxing. "I definitely shouldn't have been wearing a skirt. Sorry about that."

When my grandmother and Jacy arrived shortly thereafter, Alison immediately set them to work opening bags of wasabi peas and roasted nuts and putting them in little ramekins. She'd presented me with parchment paper I was meant to roll into cones and fill with crudités, which I had been forbidden to cut without supervision, as she didn't want them "clunky and trite." After about half an hour, Jacy was washing mesclun in a barrel, Mormor was boiling more eggs, and I was filling additional ramekins with chutneys, béarnaise sauce, honey-mustard, and ketchup

(Alison's menu included unorthodox nods to my parents' favorite foods, which in the case of my father meant hot dogs). Apparently Alison felt safe assigning me to fill things. Alison herself was standing at the sink over a massive cutting board, drowning in an apron that more closely resembled a tent. She turned, wielding a knife as long as her arm, and surveyed the kitchen with evident satisfaction.

"That's good, Jacy," she nodded, "but transfer that batch to the draining rack. We don't want it to be soggy." I could see Jacy open her mouth, reconsider, and close it again. Alison walked over to where Mormor was now tackling cilantro. "Come on, Mormor," she said. "I told you I need that to be minced, not chopped." Mormor moved the pile she'd set aside back onto the chopping board and started in on it again. As Alison turned to investigate what I considered my first-rate performance with the condiment containers, I glanced in Mormor's direction and was pretty sure that she winked at me. "Keep going," was all I got, and Alison headed back to the sink, holding her knife in the air like Lady Liberty's torch, as straight-backed and watchful as the statue herself.

I have always known I was fortunate in my family overall, in the myriad subtle ways we support and encourage each other. I was immensely grateful to see that afternoon, with the three of us sucking up orders and criticism from Alison as she masterfully whipped up dozens of platters of varied hors d'oeuvres and a full buffet, that I was not the only one enjoying watching Alison assume total control.

A few hours later the guests began to arrive. A family friend had generously offered to be the emcee, and about an hour into the party, while my parents were circulating and greeting guests, he suggested it would be a good time for Alison and me to make some welcoming remarks. For almost a year I had anticipated this moment but had hurled myself into the concrete aspects of planning instead of crafting an eloquent speech. I was good at the last minute, I told myself. Everything worthwhile I'd ever done had been accomplished under fire. I thrived on pressure, had a strange knack for speaking in public in spite of nerves and social awkwardness; with my loquacity and Alison's charm, we'd be fine.

As my mother squirmed in her chair, uncomfortable at finding herself the focus of so much attention, and my father beamed in the spotlight, an expression he could have peeled off Alison's face at one of her birthday parties, we walked up to the front of the room. Mr. Fox tapped on the mike, and more than a hundred people fell silent. Suddenly I realized I had nothing to say. I looked at my parents with what I hoped was a loving expression, but I was thinking: "This was the dumbest idea I ever had in my life." This bought me a few seconds, and I saw the people in the front of the crowd smiling approvingly, thinking, no doubt, what good daughters we were, anticipating a warm, funny speech, an eloquent welcome, two sisters sharing warm, funny memories accumulated over thirty-plus years in a family. Alison shifted her weight from one foot to the other. She was standing behind me and to my right; I kept turning toward her to encourage her to jump in until we formed an awkward triangle with the standing mike.

Mercifully, it was over quickly. I thanked everyone for coming, thanked my parents for being good sports, expressed my feeble wishes for everyone to get up and dance, have a good time. I kept praying for Alison to say something, *anything*, but she was frozen, her body rigid, hands clasped in front of her in a demure pose as unnatural as her silence. When I had nothing left to say, although I hadn't said much, I elbowed Alison, hard, in the rib cage. She stumbled but did not fall. Her hands remained clasped. I took one last look at my parents, imagined I saw disappointment on their faces.

"I guess I speak for Alison, too," I said.

This got my biggest, actually only, laugh, and even Alison laughed next to me, red-faced, her chin tilted down. After a few seconds during which we shuffled closer to our parents, somebody else got up at the mike, and I fled to the kitchen.

I keep thinking about that moment, the culmination of almost a year of preparation and collaboration, by far the most ambitious undertaking of our history as a team, including the time we reconstructed Boston's Beacon theater in a storage box, down to tiny pipe cleaner actors with embroidery floss wigs. Later that night in the kitchen, I cornered Alison, who was washing dishes at the enormous sink, even though I had forbidden her to hide out and leave me to talk to the guests on my own.

"Why did you do that?" I seethed.

"What?" she said innocently, shrugging her shoulders. She was relaxed then, had an audience: a number of my relatives were also seeking refuge in the kitchen.

"It was cruel and unfair," I said. "And I feel like an idiot." One of my aunts told me I did a fine job and that everybody thought so, which may have been true, but I was still furious with Alison, whose lack of concern for my stress level apparently knew no bounds. When the party was over and we had spent hours cleaning up with the help of a few saintly friends, we were still not speaking, and she marched out the front door without so much as a good-bye.

The next morning, when she showed up at our parents' house to pick up her cooking supplies, I was sitting on the patio steps, cradling a big cup of coffee.

"Excuse me," she said, nudging my shoulder with her leg to pass by, and I grabbed hold of her ankle. She shook free of my hand and moved on toward the house. "Hey," she added, just before she opened the door. "Your speech was pretty good last night." I couldn't tell whether she was being sarcastic.

JANUARY 25, 2003: IT IS ALISON'S THIRTY-SECOND birthday party, and as Alison has taken the gauntlet from my mother—who created fairy-tale birthday parties for us each year until we were too old to want them—her last few have been, to put it mildly, grand affairs. This one, like most, has a theme: Alice in Wonderland (last year's was Elvis). The theme was made manifest in the invitations, which were folded neatly, in thirds, into blood-red envelopes designed to stand out in the mailbox, and featured a surreal, possibly opium-induced scene of the Mad Hatter's tea, with Alison's face superimposed on some of the guests' bodies, an interesting notion if you stop to think about it. Alison not only has no computer skills; she has no computer, so I suspect I will be meeting at this party, at the very least, a graphic designer and an illustrator. It is, of course, just as likely that someone she works with at the catering company has a cousin who owns a stationery shop on the Cape and that Alison offered to make this cousin's child a wedding cake shaped like a lobster complete with marzipan claws as a trade for the professional services. Regardless, the invitations arrive early (shocking), with no directions (not so shocking) and an outright plea for gifts and alcoholic beverages (wholly anticipated), which is a special Alison touch for any and every occasion. She would not get away with this so readily if her own gift giving was not marginally out of control. I would not be surprised in a given year, for example, to receive a Veterans Day package wrapped in army-green cellophane, or a mixed tape in honor of the Fourth of July. On my thirtieth birthday Alison gave me thirty discrete presents, each wrapped in a different paper, cloth, or foil, and, as I opened each one, explained the circumstances under which she'd chosen it.

Alison believes a party should include everybody and

his neighbor's ex-wife, and if everybody doesn't get along with everybody else, that's the guests' loss; she'll have fun either way. To my constant astonishment, her strategy rarely backfires, and at Alison-sponsored events I always find myself standing with a plate of the best food I've had since her last party, observing my octogenarian grandmother deep in conversation about, say, Swedish meatballs, with a flamboyant gay bartender from London wearing tight red leather pants. Or my dad—outfitted from head to toe in casual Brooks Brothers—listening intently as a devout Buddhist with a nose ring and only one name describes her latest sculpture of a centaur, or her part-time work as a nude model at the art school up the street.

The general arc of Alison's adult birthday parties is a slow and mellow start, family and close friends only, albeit with a full bar and bartender, a four- or five-course meal, passed hors d'oeuvres—think one-sip portions of three contrasting soups—and decorations befitting a photo shoot for a food magazine. I believe, although I should confirm this, that Alison once actually painted her entire apartment in honor of her birthday; the existing color scheme simply didn't match her vision for the night. After an hour or two of mingling, the older relatives and family friends depart for the suburbs, and the real fun, or debauchery, begins.

To help you imagine the size of the guest list, I think it's safe to say that Alison knows more people than my ten closest friends combined, none of whom qualify as shy. So when I say crowd, I mean crowd: I mean dancing with a DJ (if you have as many friends as Alison does, you can always arrange for details such as DJs at cost), a wait-staff, some of whom bear a strong family resemblance to the guest of honor, and a handful of animals, most of whom belong to someone on the premises.

Two years ago at her house in Boston, the birthday frenzy reached an apotheosis when I heard a rumor that Alison's friends wanted our non–peer-group relatives to leave the party before ten. I checked with one of my cousins, who confirmed that she, too, had heard this rumor and wanted to know if I had ever hosted a party large enough for a rumor to spread, as she had not and was feeling kind of bad about it. There was no time to indulge in party envy, however, as my aunt Linnea and grandmother appeared, faces flushed, eyes bright, to alert us to the fact that they were refusing to leave.

"I didn't ask you to leave," I said, starting to get confused. "And I don't know why you're supposed to." My grandmother folded her arms across her chest, planted her feet.

"I know," she said, with a dignity only eight decades–plus of living could conjure up. "We *all* know. And we're staying."

My cousin and I were clued in pretty quickly when someone shouted that the cops had arrived, and everybody flocked to the entryway and down the staircase to witness what was sure to be a showdown between Alison and the Dorchester police force, or whatever segment of it they had sent along to deal with what was probably a run-of-the-mill noise complaint.

"I'd put my money on Alison," one of her friends whispered behind me, in response to speculation from another friend that a fight might ensue. I resisted turning around and saying that although Alison could certainly take on a few police officers in ordinary circumstances, I'd put *my* money on my mother, who could prevent Alison from so much as raising her voice in the presence of the law, and in any other situation, with one narrowed eye and a barely audible clearing of the throat. My mother has always been the one person able to subdue Alison; she's like an Alison-whisperer, with Alison as the wild bucking horse just waiting for a formidable opponent to show up and tame her. "That's only *one* cop," my cousin whispered, as my parents, aunts and uncles, and grandmother pushed through Alison's friends to get a better view. "Oh my God," she said. "Only. One. Cop," as I, too, realized what was happening, or rather what was about to. I would say the most surreal moment of my albeit relatively sheltered life was hearing my grandmother plaintively asking people to move aside so she could have a better view. If you've never watched your father watch a "policeman" in a silk thong give your sister a lap dance, I don't recommend you seek the experience out. Alison will be angry if I don't clarify the situation as follows: her friends had ordered the stripper; she knew nothing about it and was mortified that her family was there to witness the show.

But back to Alice. When I opened Alison's invitation in my elevator, I had not thought about *Alice in Wonderland* in years. As I idly picked out the Alison faces in the swirly design of the tea party, I found myself thinking about *Through the Looking Glass*, the lesser-known sequel to Lewis Carroll's classic, which is even more bizarre and twisted and surreal. My grandparents had owned a dusty, leather-bound copy, which I discovered one day at the bottom of a shelf in their living room and read in one gulp, lying in front of the fireplace. I read *Alice in Wonderland* afterward, took it out of the library, but the fall down the rabbit hole never took hold for me like the passing into— and then right through—that sinister mirror.

At the time I didn't think much about why Alison had chosen this theme. I knew why she'd chosen Elvis— my family is mildly obsessed with the King, including dueling impressions and one actual pair of blue suede shoes, and I've often wondered if Alison in particular sympathized with his uncontrollable appetites and public weight struggles, as well as the emergence of "fat Elvis," late in his life. I did remember, though, as I surveyed the invitation, something I had forgotten from twenty years before. When as a ten-year-old I read what I considered a pale follow-up to *Through the Looking Glass*, I started to play around with the book's title, almost unconsciously. I have always liked combining words, making new words out of existing ones, and, in my mind, I transformed *Alice in Wonderland* into Alison Wonderland; I liked my modified version because Alison's middle name is Joy, which to me fit nicely with *wonder* and made me a little jealous as to the lack of possibilities for my own prosaic middle name. I couldn't remember if I ever told Alison about my revised title, but I doubted it had been the inspiration for her theme. I forgot to ask her, forgot about the party's theme altogether, in fact, until I arrived at her new apartment in Boston's South End with my friend Nicole and was met at the front door by a tiny blond in a daringly short, pale blue Betsey Johnson dress with a white lace collar and sash.

"Welcome to the Mad Hatter's tea party," Alison greeted us, cackling in appropriately mad fashion and shoving us into the main room, where many of my relatives, crowded around a laden coffee table, were probably placing quiet bets as to the possible appearance of a drag queen this time, for variety. "Don't I look mahhhvelous?"

Before I could tell her to lay off the act or take in her outfit, which she would never have called a costume, I had to take in her new place. Alison is one of those people who luck into good apartments the way some people always find money in their coat pockets, although some of this is not luck at all but the result of her rare ability to look at a bare, dingy room and see a glittering palace of possibility. With the dizzying effect that is characteristic of her style, my eyes were drawn both down and up: down to the vintage fabric she'd salvaged from my mother's ancient sewing drawer and spread out like a Middle Eastern carpet in the main room, number one on the list of fifty things I never would have thought to do if this particular apartment had been mine to decorate. On the ceiling a hundred paper flowers in a rainbow of colors were suspended from invisible string, more Garden of Eden than Wonderland, but lush and exotically beautiful. On one wall she'd hung an enormous gold-framed mirror, the kind I love but am too cheap to buy, although I refrain from pointing this out because I know she will have a long, boring story about how someone she knows at some gallery was hauling the mirror out to an alley and scratched it on one corner and she got it for free. On the mirror she'd taped or otherwise affixed a full deck of cards, number sides out, as though someone had thrown them at the mirror and they'd stuck. Through the first half of the party I found myself catching little fragments of my reflection around the cards and wondering why they were there. I had written them off as an eclectic Alison touch, when one of her friends passed me a platter of shrimp cocktail saying, "It's cool she remembered the cards. Makes me want to read the book again."

Oh *yeah*, I thought. *Alice in Wonderland*. The Queen of Hearts and all those other suites playing croquet. I wandered back to the bar, which of course was in Alison's bedroom, because who wouldn't want a full bar in her bedroom, bottles of liquor and wine arranged on gold-lace-rimmed trays, like giant perfume bottles in amber and aqua and green. Spotting rows of color halfway up the wall to the left of the bar, I pushed closer through a throng of people only to realize it was a wall of candy, something straight out of *Willy Wonka and the Chocolate*

Factory. I'd never seen so much candy before outside a store and rarely in one. There is a penny candy place near my parents' house that has jars like these, with lids on the tops, and Alison and I used to ride our bikes there when we were kids, which maybe is where she got the idea, but still I found myself thinking: Who would do this? Who would even come up with such an idea?

The crowd parted and suddenly Alison was standing next to me.

"I call it the Candy Store," she explained, adjusting her Alice headband. "I have all your favorites," she added conspiratorially. "You know how this family likes candy." I nodded, slowly. This was true. Almost without exception the relatives on my mother's side are candy fanatics, and I noticed a few of them within my line of vision holding red plastic cups full of licorice sticks or gumdrops or Gummi bears.

I thought about everything I had read about gastric bypass surgery and sugar and digestion. I thought of Alison lying at night in her enormous bed, piled high with velvet cushions and a few salvaged childhood bears, five feet away from this wall of candy, whose pull she has never been able to resist. I folded my lips into a seam in my equally tight face. This is what I thought then: Why would you have all that candy around when it could so easily make you sick? Why would you build a wall of temptation for yourself in your own bedroom? But realizing even in the moment how perfectly the wall of candy encapsulated the even mixture of exasperation and envy

Alison never failed to churn up in me, I also thought: that's the coolest, most outrageous thing I've ever seen in anyone's house.

"Alison," I started, in spite of my clenched teeth. I couldn't help myself. Neither could she. She interrupted me before I could finish.

"Especially *your* favorites, though. I know what you like, and everything's there. I bought those first."

Alison spent much of the night seated at a table she had put up in the little loft space in front of the big window in her living room, elevated five or six feet from the rest of the room, which has the effect of a miniature stage. There was a second chair at this table, and every time I looked up, she was holding court with a different friend, sipping champagne, waving a shrimp in the air by its tail for emphasis. I managed to snag an armchair in the living room, which I refused to abandon because seating was so limited, and there appeared to be some kind of dirty-dancing contest that I hoped to avoid. Beside me, Nicole was actually knitting, ensuring that we not only seemed older and less scintillating than the rest of the guests in our age group but were actually approaching geriatric. At one point my grandmother passed me a stack of photographs, and I took them.

"Wow. She looks like a different person now," one of her new friends commented, peering at the top picture, Alison at her maximum weight standing with one arm outstretched by a cake covered with daffodils and tulips.

The other pictures were linked only by the fact that they had been taken during this same period of Alison's life, and I looked around to see if anybody else found this bizarre—that we were passing around images of Alison, at her most overweight, to compare them to the way she looked now—but nobody else seemed to notice. Then I looked for Alison, who had come down from her platform, to see what she thought, but she was already holding up one of the pictures herself.

"I look *disgusting*," she proclaimed, a little gleeful, and I passed the pile I was holding to the person on my right without flipping through the stack. If Alison was going to regard her former self with such loathing, I couldn't change her mind, but I didn't have to play along. I wondered who she saw when she looked at these pictures from her past, if she was even seeing my sister, seeing herself.

Later, after most of our relatives had gone home, I found myself watching Alison on her stage, the way I often find myself watching Alison, as I have watched Alison all of her life. Someone had given her a tiara, which she was wearing on top of her headband. Our eyes met and locked. She smiled at me, and for a moment it was as though there was nobody else in the room.

"Are you having fun?" she mouthed, as a Prince song came on the stereo, and her companion on the stage jumped down, presumably to start dancing.

"Yes," I mouthed back, and I was. It is fun watching Alison have fun. It always has been.

IT IS NOT UNTIL I AM BACK IN NEW YORK ON THE MONDAY after Alison's party and buy myself a paperback version of *Alice in Wonderland* that I remember much about it beyond the classic scenes: the cards, the Cheshire cat, Tweedledum and Tweedledee, and, of course, the tea party she'd re-created on the invitations. As it turns out, Alice has an older sister, who had never made any kind of impression on me; discovering her wasn't a memory triggered but an introduction. At the very beginning of the story, Alice is having a lackluster picnic in a meadow with this older sister, who won't stop reading her book to play with Alice, who is left fiddling idly with a deck of cards. It is Alice's huff at her sister's indifference that leads to her fall down the rabbit hole. Like the *Wizard of Oz*, which incorporates people and objects from Dorothy's everyday life into her dramatic visit to Oz, *Alice in Wonderland* features creatures and objects from Alice's life in a Freudian dreamscape capable of transforming a two-dimensional card into a three-dimensional villainess in a world with no seeming dimensions at all.

This makes me wonder if Alison sees her new life, her thin self, as a dream from which she might someday wake up, or if she now sees her old self, her fat self, as a dream she had long ago and hopes never to revisit. When I look back on it afterward, I see that her apartment itself has a fairy-tale quality, with the patterned fabric like an Arabian carpet and the sky full of flowers and touches of gold, and Alison's homemade raspberry vodka glistening ruby all over the room. At the party, the bottles of vodka had tags tied to their necks that read, "Drink me," in Alison's block writing, which she uses for labeling. It is, of course, the "Drink me" bottle that causes Alice to grow and then shrink and then grow again. I wonder if there is symbolism to this, too: the provision of a potion—not one, but dozens, all over the room—that promises change.

These days I no longer get passed diet tips or weight-loss strategies on Alison's behalf. Instead I get a question, which I have now been asked, truly, by almost every single person I know: "Do you feel jealous of Alison now that she is thin too?" Like many questions, I think this says more about the asker than it does about either Alison or me. Most people consider weight an essential factor in the mix that comprises the self. You hear this all the time: people tend to "feel better" thin, "hate themselves" fat, as though the size of their bodies were some sort of mood barometer, determining factor. Alison and I both made this mistake for many years, made it over and over again.

I will say this. Now that there is no longer a wall dividing our bedrooms, or two hundred pounds between us, there is a new lightness to our relationship, not an ease or tolerance or understanding, but a lightness—it is the only word that expresses the quality of the change. I would like to talk about how we are now model sisters, laughing at the old days when I sealed her mouth closed with duct tape, swapping stories about the time she locked me out of the house in a lightning storm or when I put her favorite stuffed bear in the toilet and flushed. It wouldn't be honest, though; it wouldn't be fair to what *is*.

Sometimes I look at Alison across a table, hear her voice on the phone, and suddenly feel as though I've driven into a tunnel, someplace small and dark with no discernible end. Within a matter of hours in each other's presence, I get tense and Alison gets defensive. She starts testing me; I take the bait.

"Do you and Alison still fight?" a friend asked me the other day, as though it was not Alison's body changed but her personality excised, and mine neutered somehow in the process. I opened my mouth to respond and then shut it again, imagining what Alison's answer would be.

"Yes," I say, leaving it at that.

I SUSPECT I AM NOT THE ONLY READER WHO HAS forgotten the very end of *Alice in Wonderland*. When Alice returns from her adventures, her head is resting in the lap of her older sister, the one whose role in the book is simply to *be* Alice's older sister, a role perhaps more complicated than her time on the page would imply. Alice shakes herself fully awake and describes all her adventures in Wonderland, and her sister listens, kisses her and sends her in for her tea. If you remember anything about the end of this book, it is probably up to this point: Alice getting up from the grassy knoll and scampering up to the house. But the book does not quite end there. In fact, the very last scene does not include Alice at all. It reads as follows:

But her sister sat still just as she left her, leaning her head on her hand, watching the setting sun, and thinking of little Alice and all her wonderful Adventures, till she too began dreaming after a fashion, and this was her dream:—

First, she dreamed of little Alice herself, and once again the tiny hands were clasped upon her knee, and the bright eager eyes were looking up into hers—she could hear the very tones of her voice, and see that queer little toss of her head to keep back the wandering hair that *would* always get into her eyes—and still as she listened, or seemed to listen, the whole place around her became alive with the strange creatures of her little sister's dream.

The long grass rustled at her feet as the White Rabbit hurried by—the frightened Mouse splashed his way through the neighbouring pool—she could hear the rattle of the teacups as the March Hare and his friends shared their never-ending meal, and the shrill voice of the Queen ordering off her unfortunate guests to execution—once more the pig-baby was sneezing on the Duchess's knee, while plates and dishes crashed around it—once more the shriek of the Gryphon, the squeaking of the Lizard's slate-pencil, and the choking of the suppressed guinea-pigs, filled the air, mixed up with the distant sobs of the miserable Mock Turtle.

So she sat on, with closed eyes, and half believed herself in Wonderland, though she knew she had but to open them again, and all would change to dull reality—the grass would be only rustling in the wind, and the pool rippling to the waving of the reeds—the rattling teacups

would change to tinkling sheep-bells, and the Queen's
shrill cries to the voice of the shepherd boy—and the
sneeze of the baby, the shriek of the Gryphon, and all the
other queer noises, would change (she knew) to the confused clamour of the busy farm-yard—while the lowing
of the cattle in the distance would take the place of the
Mock Turtle's heavy sobs.

Lastly, she pictured to herself how this same little sister
of hers would, in the after-time, be herself a grown woman;
and how she would keep, through all her riper years, the
simple and loving heart of her childhood: and how she
would gather about her other little children, and make
their eyes bright and eager with many a strange tale, perhaps even with the dream of Wonderland of long ago:
and how she would feel with all their simple sorrows, and
find a pleasure in all their simple joys, remembering her
own child-life, and the happy summer days.

Lewis Carroll, born Charles Lutwidge Dodgson, was a
firstborn, the oldest of eleven. I did not know this until I
looked it up after Alison's birthday party, but it didn't
surprise me at all.

NOT SO LONG AGO I HEARD SOMEONE DESCRIBE ALISON
as "a shadow of her former self" and had to turn away so
as not to laugh in this person's face. A shadow? I would
imagine that even Alison's shadow would be loud if given
a voice, have more presence than most people's flesh-

and-blood bodies. If Alison gets to be so thin she is barely visible from a side view, I will still take issue with this description: Alison is the most real, three-dimensional person I know, regardless of the breadth of her dimensions.

Do I speak for Alison? Sometimes, but only when she refuses to. I don't mind much, and like Alison, I blow over easy. In the long run, I think it's a pretty fair trade, which is, in my mind, the most you can ask of a sister. In our case I make the footsteps, make them straight and clean and easy to step in, even in inclement weather, whitecaps of snow. And every so often, she lets me veer off the path, walk down the middle of the street without looking over my shoulder. You might even say she gives me a glimpse into Wonderland.

acknowledgments

I am so grateful for the opportunity to work with the very best: Jennifer Barth, who is all I dreamed an editor could be, and Amanda Urban, who always knows what to do.

Many thanks as well to Carolyn Ebbitt, Nicole La Borde, Bryant Palmer, and Caroline Suh for their invaluable input; Ben Hohn for his unflagging support and enthusiasm; Sandra and Joel Wilensky for pretty much everything; and most of all Alison Wilensky, who knew I could—and should—write this book, even when I did not, and who continues to influence me more than she knows.

about the author

AMY WILENSKY is a graduate of Vassar College and Columbia University's MFA writing program. Her first book, *Passing for Normal*, was nominated for a National Book Award. A native of suburban Boston, she lives in New York City with her husband, Ben.